Mediterranean Kalorik Maxx Air Fryer Oven Cookbook

600-Day Healthy Recipes for Smart People to Fry, Roast, Bake, and Grill on a Budget

Wird Buckey

© Copyright 2021 Wird Buckey - All Rights Reserved.

In no way is it legal to reproduce, duplicate, or transmit any part of this document by either electronic means or in printed format. Recording of this publication is strictly prohibited, and any storage of this material is not allowed unless with written permission from the publisher. All rights reserved.

The information provided herein is stated to be truthful and consistent, in that any liability, regarding inattention or otherwise, by any usage or abuse of any policies, processes, or directions contained within is the solitary and complete responsibility of the recipient reader. Under no circumstances will any legal liability or blame be held against the publisher for any reparation, damages, or monetary loss due to the information herein, either directly or indirectly.

Respective authors own all copyrights not held by the publisher.

Legal Notice:

This book is copyright protected. This is only for personal use. You cannot amend, distribute, sell, use, quote or paraphrase any part of the content within this book without the consent of the author or copyright owner. Legal action will be pursued if this is breached.

Disclaimer Notice:

Please note the information contained within this document is for educational and entertainment purposes only. Every attempt has been made to provide accurate, up-to-date and reliable, complete information. No warranties of any kind are expressed or implied. Readers acknowledge that the author is not engaging in the rendering of legal, financial, medical or professional advice.

By reading this document, the reader agrees that under no circumstances are we responsible for any losses, direct or indirect, which are incurred as a result of the use of information contained within this document, including, but not limited to, errors, omissions, or inaccuracies.

Table of Contents

Introduction 6
Chapter-1: Understanding the Mediterranean Diet 7
    What Is the Mediterranean Diet? 7
    The History of The Mediterranean Diet 7
    Benefits of The Mediterranean Diet 8
Chapter 2: Why to Use Kalorik Digital Maxx Air Fryer Oven? 10
    Kalorik Digital Maxx Air Fryer Oven Deconstructed 11
    How to use Kalorik Digital Maxx Air Fryer Oven 13
    Cooking and Adjustment 14
    Cleaning and Maintenance 14
Chapter 3: Meal Plan for 21 Days 16
Chapter 4: Breakfast Recipes 20
    Mini Veggie Frittatas 20
    Beef Frittata 22
    Oats Granola 23
    Turkey & Zucchini Omelet 24
    Eggs with Chicken & Kale 25
    Sausage & Pancetta Omelet 26
Chapter 5: Beef Recipes 27
    Sweet & Spicy Beef Jerky 27
    Spiced Sirloin Steak 29
    Herbed Flank Steak 30
    Seasoned Rib-Eye Steak 31
    Simple Beef Sirloin Roast 32
    Spicy Beef Chuck Roast 33
    Seasoned Beef Tenderloin 34
    Spicy Beef Top Roast 35
Chapter 6: Lamb Recipes 36
    Nut-Crusted Rack of Lamb 36
    Herbed Lamb Loin Chops 38

Cheesy Lamb Burgers	39
Glazed Lamb Meatballs	41
Maple Glazed Lamb Chops	43
Mustard Lamb Chops	44
Herbed Leg of Lamb	45
Spicy Lamb Burgers	46

Chapter 7: Pork Recipes 47

Herbed Pork Chops	47
Seasoned Pork Shoulder	49
Simple Pork Chops	50
Glazed Ham	51
Spicy Pork Tenderloin	52
Simple Pork Loin	53
Pork Taco Casserole	54
Honey Glazed Pork Tenderloin	55

Chapter 8: Poultry Recipes 56

Stuffed Roasted Chicken	56
Crispy Chicken Breasts	58
Herbed Cornish Hen	59
Beer Coated Duck Breast	60
Spicy Roasted Chicken	61
Buttered Turkey Breast	62
Garlicky Duck Legs	63
Simple Turkey Breast	64
Herbed Chicken Thighs	65
Glazed Chicken Drumsticks	66

Chapter 9: Fish & Seafood Recipes 67

Trout with Broccoli	67
Herbed Salmon	69
Tangy Sea Bass	70
Glazed Salmon	71
Cajun Spiced Salmon	72

Buttered Salmon	73
Shrimp Burgers	74
Rosemary Tilapia	75
Halibut & Shrimp with Pasta	76
Sweet & Sour Halibut	78

Chapter 10: Vegetarian Recipes **79**

Buttered Zucchini	79
Buttered Broccoli	80
Buttered Asparagus	81
Balsamic Green Beans	82
Tofu with Broccoli	83
Glazed Mushrooms	84
Lemony Okra	85
Spiced Sweet Potatoes	86
Spiced Cauliflower	87
Lemony Brussels Sprout	88

Chapter 11: Dessert Recipes **89**

Raspberry Danish	89
Blueberry Muffins	91
Lemon Mousse	93
Chocolate Brownies	94
Fruity Crumble	95
Glazed Banana	96
Cranberry Cupcakes	97
Apple Crisp	99
Zucchini Mug Cake	100
Blackberry Cobbler	101

Conclusion **103**

Introduction

Mediterranean Kalorik Maxx Air Fryer Oven Cookbook amazingly easy recipes to fry, roast, bake, and grill with your Kalorik Maxx Air Fryer Oven! The Kalorik Maxx Air Fryer Oven is an easy way to cook delicious healthy meals. Rather than cooking the food in oil and hot fat that may affect your health, the machine uses rapid hot air to circulate around and cook meals. This allows the outside of your food to be crispy and also makes sure that the inside layers are cooked through.

Kalorik Maxx Air Fryer Oven allows us to cook almost everything and a lot of dishes. We can use the air fryer oven to cook meat, vegetables, fruit, and fish. It is possible to prepare your entire Mediterranean meals, starting from appetizers to main courses.

Chapter-1: Understanding the Mediterranean Diet

What Is the Mediterranean Diet?

When studied historically the Mediterranean diet can be tied to a specific region or era. But scientifically proven the Mediterranean diet taken a much universally place in human history. Due to its unique approach to food consumption, it brings more balance to our diet and fills our plate with a healthy nutritional meal in a proportionate amount. It is an innate human need to consume food of all sorts, ranging from protein-rich meats to the fiber loaded vegetables, and fruits and the carb filled grains. So, this diet only works in light of such need. Its emphasis more on clean fats and healthy oils for daily consumption. The diet carried its name from its origin, which is rooted in the region around the Mediterranean Sea. People from those places were more reliant on seafood, fresh vegetables, fruits, olive oil, and whole grains. Their approach rightly guided the world to a nutrient-rich meal plan.

The greatest thing about the Mediterranean diet is it does not only guarantee good health, but it comes with so much flavor, aroma, and colors for our platters. Unlike, other restrictive diets, the Mediterranean diet is much more open and flexible. It suggests so many delectable options for every taste palate that it is easy for anyone to adopt. Over the course of time, the Mediterranean diet has significantly evolved according to different regions and culinary cultures. Today, it manages to prevent and cure several life-threatening diseases.

The History of The Mediterranean Diet

The Mediterranean diet that exists today originated from the stretches of Greece and Italy. Different classes of those societies individually contributed to the formation of this diet. There was a great inclination towards the eating of white omega rich meat including all seafood. Along with that, they use to consume lots of vegetables, fruits, and grains in some amount. The typical food patterns of the people in those areas were adopted readily by many due to the diversity of the nutrients the Mediterranean pyramid has provided. Over the years it existed as a culinary tradition, it was not until 1975 when American biologist Ansel keys and Margaret key collaborated to publicize the Mediterranean diet as a health-oriented meal plan. However, its widespread recognition came late in the 1990s. Studies regarding the benefits of this diet were conducted in Madrid and Naples; the objective data obtained revealed significant results. This study confirms the wide-ranging effects of the Mediterranean diet over people's health which were predicted decades ago. Later scientists came up with their different versions of the Mediterranean diet, but the one which was readily adopted was given by Walter Willet and his colleagues in mid-1990s. This approach was closest to the naturally evolved Mediterranean diet. It suggests a similar pattern of food intake as the people from ancient Greece did.

Benefits of The Mediterranean Diet

A healthy diet can do miracles no medicine can guarantee. Mediterranean diet is no less than miraculous if we acknowledge the great benefits it brings to human health. Besides accelerating the rate of metabolism and detoxifying the body from harmful oxidants, this diet can deal with a range of mental and physical ailments including cancer, cardiovascular disorders, and Parkinson, etc.

1. **Prevent Alzheimer and Parkinson:**

Both Parkinson and Alzheimer are neural disorders which result from the toxic build up in the brain and damage caused by it. The Mediterranean diet has shown unbelievable effects over the patients of Parkinson and Alzheimer, and they all experience improved mental functioning because of this diet plan.

2. **Fights Against Cardiovascular Diseases:**

All the cardiovascular diseases are linked with high blood cholesterol levels or weakening of the cardiac muscles. With the Mediterranean diet, such threats can be fought due to its good fat content. It does not allow the accumulation of bad fats and toxins in the body while keeping the metabolism active and running all the time.

3. **Lowers Bad Cholesterol:**

The olive oil based Mediterranean diet is free from all the saturated fats. Resultantly it is low on bad cholesterol. This form of cholesterol is responsible for blocking the blood vessels and causes a high blood cholesterol level.

4. **High Life Expectancies:**

Good diet and longevity have a very real connection. The better you eat, the healthier you stay. When you eat everything and balance, it can guarantee a long life. This fact is happened to be true for people consuming a Mediterranean diet, and therefore it is prescribed to everyone looking for higher life expectancy.

5. **Aids Cancer Treatment:**

Another curse of the current age is incurable cancer and the like diseases. Where most of the medicinal and chemical therapies fail to cure the disease, a change in diet have proven miraculous for most of the cancer patients. Mediterranean diet has been proven the most beneficial in this regard. People who are already consuming this diet shows about a sixty percent lesser tendency of developing cancer than the people who don't consume it.

Chapter 2: Why to Use Kalorik Digital Maxx Air Fryer Oven?

Being a Kalorik appliance is already a pretty big reason to bring this beauty home. But there are actual cooking advantages that this efficient Maxx Air Fryer Oven offers you.

1. **Modern Design**

The design of the Maxx Air Fryer oven is something that makes it stand out among the rest of the air fryer ovens in the market. Its size and shape make a complete balance; you can manage cooking space and your countertop space at the same time. Since this oven can replace multiple food appliances due to a variety of its cooking functions, it can be easily placed anywhere in the kitchen.

2. **Multifunctional**

This one appliance can replace most of the cooking appliances in your kitchen as it provides a number of cooking functions in one place. This Air Fryer oven can be used to bake food, toast, grill, roast, braise, rotisserie, broil, and dehydrate all sorts of food items. The versatility of its cooking function increases when you count the temperature and timer settings, which can also be adjusted manually to cook according to your own preferences. There are several accessories that come with the oven, and they all help to cook on a specific cooking mode. There is a total of 21 preset given in the appliance which allows you to cook all variety of meals.

3. **Modern French Door System**

One of the most interesting features of this Air fryer oven is its French door system, which opens from the center with a single-hand opening. Due to this feature, there is no dripping and scalding on its door during each cooking session. The French door system also makes it easy to check the food or to handle it during cooking. Moreover, it provides you complete space to insert a large tray or pan inside the Air Fryer oven.

4. **Family Size**

The 26-quart Maxx Air fryer oven is known for its large size and all the capacity suitable for cooking all portion sizes. So, whether you have a large family or a small family, this Air fryer oven can serve the needs of all. Now baking a turkey and roasting a whole chicken or a duck is not a problem, as you can not only adjust them all in this Air Fryer oven, but you can also add side ingredients along with them.

5. **Simple and Smart Control Panel**

Another good feature of this Air Fryer oven is its easy and simple control panel, which is completely user friendly. There are two main buttons to choose between the Air Fryer options or baking options. And the control dial is used to select the mode of cooking in each option.

Kalorik Digital Maxx Air Fryer Oven Deconstructed

The modern glass French door design of the Maxx Air Fryer is fairly simple and easy to handle. When you unbox the appliance, you will find the following parts and components inside:

Parts and Components

Firstly, there is this base unit, which has dimensions equal to 15.75" width x 12.5" length x 14" height, and inside the unit, there is 26-quart volume to hold your food items. This oven unit has sturdy built, and it must be placed on a flat, rigid and strong base. The glass door is attached to the front, and on top of the glass doors, there is a control panel and display screen. Inside the oven, there are four grooves on each sidewall to fix baking trays, dripping pans, and Air fryer basket.

The Nine Accessories

Besides the base unit, there are nine accessories that are provided with the oven to aid different cooking functions. These accessories include the following:

- Air frying basket
- Baking pan
- Air rack
- Crumb tray
- Bacon tray
- Steak/dehydrator tray
- Rotisserie spit
- Rack handle
- Rotisserie handle

All these accessories are dishwasher safe, can be removed and washed after the cooking session.

Control Panel and Cooking Functions

The control panel is fixed on the front of the appliance, on top. And it has a dial, five buttons, and a display screen. On this screen, you can see all the 21 presets written on the screen indicating different food types like:

- Chicken
- Fish
- Ribs
- Steak
- Wings
- Bacon
- Eggs
- Fries
- Corn
- Shrimp
- Vegetables
- Pizza
- Pastry etc.

Then there are other cooking modes like:

- Air Fry
- Bake
- Broil
- Roast
- Toast
- Defrost
- Reheat

The lowermost rectangular button on the control panel is labeled as START/STOP, so you can press the button to initiate or stop your cooking operations. Above this button, there are two buttons, which light up when they are pressed:

- Air Fry: When it is pressed, the appliance converts into an Air Fry. The dial is then used to select the required preset to select the time and temperature according to the recipe.
- Oven: When this button is pressed, you can use the appliance like an electric oven, and with the help you the dial, you can use the presets for an oven function.

Above the Air Fryer button, there is a button for Convection, which can be pressed to circulate the heat inside the oven through Convection. The other button on its right side is for the Light inside the oven. It can be pressed to see the condition of the food.

How to use Kalorik Digital Maxx Air Fryer Oven

Here are a few simple steps to use your Kalorik Digital Maxx Air Fryer Oven:

1. **Getting Started**

At first, place the appliance at an appropriate place in the kitchen. The back and top of the oven should be kept open for ventilation. Check all its accessories and then plug it in. The lights of the display screen will light up.

If you are using the oven for the first time, make sure to wash all the accessories with water or soap water and allow them to dry and keep them at a place where they are safe from the dirt and grease.

2. **Setting Up the oven**

The crumb tray is placed at the bottom of the oven, and it is important to use this tray to protect the floor of the oven. So always fix the crumb tray in the lowermost portion of the oven. You can now select the accessories according to the recipe and the type of food. The air fryer basket is used to Air Fry variety of food items, so use this basket to keep the food inside the oven. The baking pan and tray can be used for a variety of purpose:

- To bake food
- To roast items
- To Broil
- To toast

The Rotisserie rod and handle are provided to cook on the chicken, or duck, etc. on the rotisserie. In this way, the chicken or duck is heated properly from all sides as the rod rotates and gets an even brown color on all sides.

The dehydrator tray is used for dehydrating meat, fruits, and vegetables. And there is also a bacon tray that is used for cooking crispy bacon in the oven. You can use the accessories according to your needs. There is also an Air Rack, which you can use for Air frying as well as for roasting or baking etc.

Cooking and Adjustment

Now that you have selected the desired accessories for cooking. Prepare your food and keep it ready for the oven. The oven quickly attains the required heat for cooking, so it is suggested to not to preheat the oven and directly place the food inside and then select the cooking functions. You can adjust the settings according to the given recipe. Generally, it is best to select after your food is placed inside.

Once the food is set inside, close the French glass doors to seal the oven and then select any of the two options: AIR FRY or OVEN, then use the dial to select the required preset to adjust the time and temperature. When the appliance starts actual cooking, the timer starts ticking, and you will notice the magic happening inside the oven through its glass doors. If you want to flip or toss the food inside the oven, then simply press STOP to pause the cooking function and flip or toss the food. Close the doors again and resume cooking by pressing the START button. You can always use the LIGHT function to check the status of your food and prevent it from burning, overcooking, or undercooking.

Once the operation is completed, the appliance will indicate so by a beep or a blink on the screen. It is wise to leave the food for 5-10 minutes in the oven and then dish out for safe and easy handling. When you are done cooking, remove the food from the oven along with all the accessories used.

Cleaning and Maintenance

No cooking appliance can work for long if it is not cleaned or maintained properly, especially an Air Fryer oven like this oven needs all the care and attention to keep it suitable for cooking clean and hygienic food. Inside the oven, when food particles or dirty accessories are left without cleaning, it can cause bacterial growth, which can then contaminate the food placed inside. So, here are few simple steps to clean the appliance after every cooking session.

1. First, unplug the appliance and remove all the trays or pans placed inside. Make sure to wear gloves or oven mittens while handling the hot trays. It is important to clean the tray and pan while they are hot to prevent all the grease and food particles stuck on them from hardening.
2. Leave the cooking appliance with its door open and allow it to cool completely.
3. Use this time to wash all the accessories used in the cooking operation. You can either wash them by lightly rub them with soap water or wash them in the dishwasher. Avoid using hard material to scrub these accessories, as they could damage their outer surface.

4. Once the accessories are washed, leave them to dry completely.
5. Now that the oven is cooled from inside out, you can take a lightly damp cloth and wipe off all the grease and food particles from the inner walls of the Air Fryer oven.
6. Use another lightly wet cloth to wipe off the doors, door handle, the control panel dial, its buttons, and the displace screen.
7. Never immerse the unit water and keep it away from liquids as well.

Chapter 3: Meal Plan for 21 Days

Day 1

Breakfast: Oats Granola

Lunch: Cheesy Lamb Burgers

Dinner: Tangy Sea Bass

Day 2:

Breakfast: Beef Frittata

Lunch: Buttered Asparagus

Dinner: Mustard Lamb Chops

Day 3:

Breakfast: Turkey & Zucchini Omelet

Lunch: Balsamic Green Beans

Dinner: Buttered Turkey Breast

Day 4:

Breakfast: Eggs with Chicken & Kale

Lunch: Lemony Brussels Sprout

Dinner: Spicy Beef Chuck Roast

Day 5:

Breakfast: Beef Frittata

Lunch: Spiced Cauliflower

Dinner: Simple Pork Loin

Day 6:

Breakfast: Mini Veggie Frittata

Lunch: Cheesy Lamb Burgers

Dinner: Glazed Chicken Drumsticks

Day 7:

Breakfast: Turkey & Zucchini Omelet

Lunch: Tofu with Broccoli

Dinner: Cajun Spiced Salmon

Day 8:

Breakfast: Beef Frittata

Lunch: Glazed Mushrooms

Dinner: Beer Coated Duck Breast

Day 9:

Breakfast: Sausage & Pancetta Omelet

Lunch: Lemony Okra

Dinner: Nut-Crusted Rack of Lamb

Day 10:

Breakfast: Eggs with Chicken & Kale

Lunch: Balsamic Green Beans

Dinner: Stuffed Roasted Chicken

Day 11:

Breakfast: Oats Granola

Lunch: Shrimp Burgers

Dinner: Pork Taco Casserole

Day 12:

Breakfast: Sausage & Pancetta Omelet

Lunch: Buttered Zucchini

Dinner: Herbed Flank Steak

Day 13:

Breakfast: Mini Veggie Frittata

Lunch: Shrimp Burgers

Dinner: Maple Glazed Lamb Chops

Day 14:

Breakfast: Turkey & Zucchini Omelet

Lunch: Buttered Broccoli

Dinner: Herbed Chicken Thighs

Day 15:

Breakfast: Eggs with Chicken & Kale

Lunch: Spicy Sweet Potatoes

Dinner: Honey Glazed Pork Tenderloin

Day 16:

Breakfast: Oats Granola

Lunch: Glazed Mushrooms

Dinner: Herbed Leg of Lamb

Day 17:

Breakfast: Mini Veggie Frittata

Lunch: Glazed Lamb Meatballs

Dinner: Trout with Broccoli

Day 18:

Breakfast: Sausage & Pancetta Omelet

Lunch: Buttered Brussels Sprout

Dinner: Seasoned Beef Tenderloin

Day 19:

Breakfast: Beef Frittata

Lunch: Lemony Okra

Dinner: Halibut & Shrimp with Pasta

Day 20:

Breakfast: Oats Granola

Lunch: Spicy Lamb Burgers

Dinner: Herbed Pork Chops

Day 21:

Breakfast: Sausage & Pancetta Omelet

Lunch: Shrimp Burgers

Dinner: Herbed Cornish Hen

Chapter 4: Breakfast Recipes

Mini Veggie Frittatas

Preparation Time: 15 minutes
Cooking Time: 17 minutes
Servings: 2

Ingredients:

- 1 tablespoon butter
- ½ of white onion, sliced thinly
- 1 cup fresh mushrooms, sliced thinly
- 1¼ cups fresh spinach, chopped
- 3 eggs
- ½ teaspoon fresh rosemary, chopped
- Salt and ground black pepper, as required
- 3 tablespoons Parmesan cheese, shredded

Method:

1. In a frying pan, melt butter over medium heat and cook the onion and mushroom for about 3 minutes.
2. Add the spinach and cook for about 2-3 minutes.
3. Remove the frying pan from heat and set aside to cool slightly.
4. Meanwhile, in a small bowl, add the eggs, rosemary, salt and black pepper and beat well.
5. Divide the beaten eggs in 2 greased ramekins evenly and top with the veggie mixture, followed by the cheese.
6. Select "Air Fry" of Kalorik Digital Air Fryer Oven and then adjust the temperature to 330 degrees F.
7. Set the timer for 12 minutes and press "Start/Stop" to begin cooking.
8. When the unit beeps to show that it is preheated, place the ramekins over the air rack and insert in the Kalorik Oven.
9. When cooking time is complete, remove the ramekins from Kalorik Oven and place onto a wire rack for about 5 minutes before serving.

Nutritional Information per Serving:

- Calories 200
- Total Fat 14.6 g
- Saturated Fat 7 g
- Cholesterol 266 mg

- Sodium 356 mg
- Total Carbs 5.4 g
- Fiber 1.5 g
- Sugar 2.4 g
- Protein 13.2 g

Beef Frittata

Preparation Time: 15 minutes
Cooking Time: 20 minutes
Servings: 4

Ingredients:

- ½ pound cooked ground beef, grease removed
- 1 cup Colby Jack cheese, shredded
- 8 eggs, beaten lightly
- 4 scallions, chopped
- 1/8 teaspoon red pepper flakes, crushed
- Salt and ground black pepper, as required

Method:

1. In a bowl, add the sausage, cheese, eggs, scallion and cayenne and mix until well combined.
2. Place the mixture into a greased baking dish.
3. Select "Air Fry" of Kalorik Digital Air Fryer Oven and then adjust the temperature to 360 degrees F.
4. Set the timer for 20 minutes and press "Start/Stop" to begin cooking.
5. When the unit beeps to show that it is preheated, place the baking dish over the air rack and insert in the Kalorik Oven.
6. When cooking time is complete, remove the baking dish from Kalorik Oven and place onto a wire rack to cool for about 5 minutes before serving.
7. Cut into 4 wedges and serve hot.

Nutritional Information per Serving:

- Calories 346
- Total Fat 21.3 g
- Saturated Fat 10.1 g
- Cholesterol 403 mg
- Sodium 382 mg
- Total Carbs 2.8 g
- Fiber 0.4 g
- Sugar 1 g
- Protein 34.6 g

Oats Granola

Preparation Time: 15 minutes
Cooking Time: 15 minutes
Servings: 8

Ingredients:

- 1/3 cup butter, melted
- 1/3 cup honey
- ½ teaspoon pure vanilla extract
- 2 cups rolled oats
- ½ cup wheat germ, toasted
- ½ cup plus 2 tablespoons dried cranberries
- 4 tablespoons pumpkin seeds, shelled
- 1 tablespoon flax seed
- ½ cup walnuts, chopped
- ½ teaspoon ground cinnamon

Method:

1. In a small bowl, add the butter and honey and mix well.
2. In a large bowl, add the remaining ingredients and mix well.
3. Add the butter mixture and mix until well combined.
4. Place the mixture into a baking pan of Kalorik Digital Air Fryer Oven.
5. Select "Air Fry" of Kalorik Digital Air Fryer Oven and then adjust the temperature to 350 degrees F.
6. Set the timer for 15 minutes and press "Start/Stop" to begin cooking.
7. When the unit beeps to show that it is preheated, place the cake pan over the air rack and insert in the Kalorik Oven.
8. When cooking time is complete, remove the baking pan from Kalorik Oven and place onto a wire rack to cool completely before serving.

Nutritional Information per Serving:

- Calories 297
- Total Fat 16.6 g
- Saturated Fat 5.9 g
- Cholesterol 20 mg
- Sodium 58 mg
- Total Carbs 31.7 g
- Fiber 4.5 g
- Sugar 12.8 g
- Protein 8 g

Turkey & Zucchini Omelet

Preparation Time: 15 minutes
Cooking Time: 35 minutes
Servings: 6

Ingredients:

- 8 eggs
- ½ cup unsweetened almond milk
- 1/8 teaspoon red pepper flakes, crushed
- Salt and ground black pepper, as required
- 1 cup cooked turkey meat, chopped
- 1 cup Monterrey Jack cheese, shredded
- ½ cup fresh scallion, chopped
- ¾ cup zucchini, chopped

Method:

1. In a bowl, add the eggs, almond milk, salt and black pepper and beat well.
2. Add the remaining ingredients and stir to combine.
3. Place the mixture into a greased baking dish.
4. Select "Bake" of Kalorik Digital Air Fryer Oven and then adjust the temperature to 315 degrees F.
5. Set the timer for 35 minutes and press "Start/Stop" to begin cooking.
6. When the unit beeps to show that it is preheated, place the baking diash over the air rack and insert in the Kalorik Oven.
7. When cooking time is complete, remove the baking dish from Kalorik Oven and place onto a wire rack to cool for about 5 minutes before serving.
8. Cut into equal-sized wedges and serve hot.

Nutritional Information per Serving:

- Calories 308
- Total Fat 20 g
- Saturated Fat 9.4 g
- Cholesterol 37 mg
- Sodium 413 mg
- Total Carbs 3.6 g
- Fiber 0.7 g
- Sugar 1.4 g
- Protein 28 g

Eggs with Chicken & Kale

Preparation Time: 15 minutes
Cooking Time: 24 minutes
Servings: 4

Ingredients:

- 1 tablespoon olive oil
- 1-pound fresh baby kale, chopped
- 4 eggs
- 8 ounces cooked chicken, chopped finely
- 4 teaspoons milk
- Salt and ground black pepper, as required
- ¼ teaspoon dried rosemary

Method:

1. In a wok, heat oil over medium heat and cook the kale for about 3-4 minutes or until just wilted.
2. Remove from the heat and transfer the cooked kale into a bowl.
3. Set aside to cool slightly.
4. Divide the cooked kale into 4 greased ramekins, followed by the chicken.
5. Crack 1 egg into each ramekin and drizzle with milk.
6. Sprinkle with salt, black pepper and rosemary.
7. Select "Air Fry" of Kalorik Digital Air Fryer Oven and then adjust the temperature to 355 degrees F.
8. Set the timer for 20 minutes and press "Start/Stop" to begin cooking.
9. When the unit beeps to show that it is preheated, place the ramekins over the air rack and insert in the Kalorik Oven.
10. When cooking time is complete, remove the ramekins from Kalorik Oven and place onto a wire rack for about 5 minutes before serving.

Nutritional Information per Serving:

- Calories 237
- Total Fat 9.7 g
- Saturated Fat 2.4 g
- Cholesterol 208 mg
- Sodium 188 mg
- Total Carbs 12.5 g
- Fiber 1.7 g
- Sugar 0.6 g
- Protein 25.6 g

Sausage & Pancetta Omelet

Preparation Time: 10 minutes
Cooking Time: 15 minutes
Servings: 2

Ingredients:

- 4 eggs
- Ground black pepper, as required
- 1 pancetta slice, chopped
- 2 breakfast sausages, chopped
- 1 onion, chopped
- 1 teaspoon fresh thyme, minced

Method:

1. In a bowl, crack the eggs and black pepper and beat well.
2. Add the remaining ingredients and gently, stir to combine.
3. Place the mixture into a small baking dish.
4. Select "Air Fry" of Kalorik Digital Air Fryer Oven and then adjust the temperature to 320 degrees F.
5. Set the timer for 15 minutes and press "Start/Stop" to begin cooking.
6. When the unit beeps to show that it is preheated, place the baking dish over the air rack and insert in the Kalorik Oven.
7. When cooking time is complete, remove the baking dish from Kalorik Oven and place onto a wire rack to cool for about 5 minutes before serving.
8. Cut into 2 wedges and serve hot.

Nutritional Information per Serving:

- Calories 366
- Total Fat 23.3 g
- Saturated Fat 6.8 g
- Cholesterol 412 mg
- Sodium 1000 mg
- Total Carbs 7.8 g
- Fiber 1.4 g
- Sugar 3 g
- Protein 35.1 g

Chapter 5: Beef Recipes

Sweet & Spicy Beef Jerky

Preparation Time: 15 minutes
Cooking Time: 3 hours
Servings: 4

Ingredients:

- ¾ pound beef round roast, trimmed
- ¼ cup low-sodium soy sauce
- ¼ cup Worcestershire sauce
- ½ tablespoon maple syrup
- 1 teaspoon liquid smoke
- ¼ teaspoon garlic powder
- ¼ teaspoon onion powder
- ½ teaspoon smoked paprika
- Ground black pepper, as required

Method:

1. In a zip-top bag, place the beef and freeze for 1-2 hours to firm up.
2. Remove from the bag and place the beef onto a cutting board.
3. With a sharp knife, cut the beef into 1/8-¼-inch strips against the grain.
4. In a large bowl, add the remaining ingredients and mix until well combined.
5. Add the steak strips and coat with the mixture generously.
6. Refrigerate to marinate for about 4-6 hours.
7. Remove the beef strips from bowl and with paper towels, pat dry them.
8. Divide the beef strips onto the dehydrator tray and arrange in an even layer.
9. Select "Dehydrate" of Kalorik Digital Air Fryer Oven and then adjust the temperature to 160 degrees F.
10. Set the timer for 3 hours and press "Start/Stop" to begin cooking.
11. When the unit beeps to show that it is preheated, insert 1 tray in the top position and another in the center position.
12. When cooking time is complete, remove the trays from Kalorik Oven and serve.

Nutritional Information per Serving:

- Calories 188
- Total Fat 6.6 g

- Saturated Fat 2.4 g
- Cholesterol 73 mg
- Sodium 1076 mg
- Total Carbs 6.1 g
- Fiber 0.1 g
- Sugar 5.6 g
- Protein 24.4 g

Spiced Sirloin Steak

Preparation Time: 10 minutes
Cooking Time: 12 minutes
Servings: 2

Ingredients:

- 2 (7-ounce) top sirloin steaks
- ½ teaspoon dried rosemary, crushed
- ½ teaspoon ground cumin
- ½ teaspoon cayenne pepper
- Salt and ground black pepper, as required

Method:

1. In a small bowl, mix together rosemary, spices, salt and black pepper.
2. Season each steak with spice mixture generously.
3. Arrange the steaks onto the greased steak tray.
4. Select "Air Fry" of Kalorik Digital Air Fryer Oven and then adjust the temperature to 400 degrees F.
5. Set the timer for 12 minutes and press "Start/Stop" to begin cooking.
6. When the unit beeps to show that it is preheated, insert the steak tray in the Kalorik Oven.
7. Flip the steaks once halfway through.
8. When cooking time is complete, remove the steaks from Kalorik oven and place onto a platter for about 5 minutes before serving.

Nutritional Information per Serving:

- Calories 373
- Total Fat 12.6 g
- Saturated Fat 4.7 g
- Cholesterol 177 mg
- Sodium 209 mg
- Total Carbs 0.7 g
- Fiber 0.3 g
- Sugar 0.1 g
- Protein 60.4 g

Herbed Flank Steak

Preparation Time: 10 minutes
Cooking Time: 12 minutes
Servings: 6

Ingredients:

- 2 tablespoons fresh lemon juice
- 2 tablespoons olive oil
- 1 teaspoon fresh rosemary, minced
- 1 teaspoon fresh thyme, minced
- 1 teaspoon fresh oregano, minced
- 1 teaspoon garlic powder
- Salt and ground black pepper, as required
- 1 (2-pound) flank steak

Method:

1. In a large bowl, mix together the lemon juice, oil, herbs, garlic powder, salt and black pepper.
2. Add the steak and coat with mixture generously.
3. Cover the bowl and place in the refrigerator for at least 1 hour.
4. Arrange the steak onto the greased steak tray.
5. Select "Broil" of Kalorik Digital Air Fryer Oven and then set the timer for 12 minutes.
6. Press "Start/Stop" to begin cooking.
7. Flip the steak once halfway through.
8. When the unit beeps to show that it is preheated, insert the steak tray in the Kalorik Oven.
9. When cooking time is complete, remove the steak from Kalorik oven and place onto a cutting board for about 5 minutes.
10. Cut the steak into desired size slices and serve.

Nutritional Information per Serving:

- Calories 338
- Total Fat 17.4 g
- Saturated Fat 6 g
- Cholesterol 83 mg
- Sodium 113 mg
- Total Carbs 0.9 g
- Fiber 0.3 g
- Sugar 0.2 g
- Protein 42.2 g

Seasoned Rib-Eye Steak

Preparation Time: 10 minutes
Cooking Time: 14 minutes
Servings: 3

Ingredients:

- 2 (8-ounce) rib-eye steaks
- 2 tablespoons olive oil
- 1 tablespoon steak seasoning
- Salt and ground black pepper, as required

Method:

1. Coat the steaks with oil and then, sprinkle with seasoning, salt and black pepper evenly.
2. Arrange the steaks onto the steak tray.
3. Select "Steak" of Kalorik Digital Air Fryer Oven and then adjust the temperature to 400 degrees F.
4. Set the timer for 14 minutes and press "Start/Stop" to begin cooking.
5. When the unit beeps to show that it is preheated, insert the steak tray in the Kalorik Oven.
6. When cooking time is complete, remove the steaks from Kalorik oven and place onto a cutting board for about 5 minutes.
7. Cut each steak into desired size slices and serve.

Nutritional Information per Serving:

- Calories 495
- Total Fat 42.8 g
- Saturated Fat 14.7 g
- Cholesterol 100 mg
- Sodium 137 mg
- Total Carbs 0 g
- Fiber 0 g
- Sugar 0 g
- Protein 26.8 g

Simple Beef Sirloin Roast

Preparation Time: 10 minutes
Cooking Time: 50 minutes
Servings: 8

Ingredients:

- 2½ pounds sirloin roast
- Salt and ground black pepper, as required

Method:

1. Rub the roast with salt and black pepper generously.
2. Place the sirloin roast into the greased baking pan.
3. Select "Roast" of Kalorik Digital Air Fryer Oven and then adjust the temperature to 350 degrees F.
4. Set the timer for 50 minutes and press "Start/Stop" to begin cooking.
5. When the unit beeps to show that it is preheated, insert the baking pan in the Kalorik Oven.
6. When cooking time is complete, remove the sirloin roast from Kalorik Oven and place onto a cutting board for about 10 minutes before slicing.
7. With a sharp knife, cut the beef roast into desired sized slices and serve.

Nutritional Information per Serving:

- Calories 301
- Total Fat 20.1 g
- Saturated Fat 8.8 g
- Cholesterol 75 mg
- Sodium 95 mg
- Total Carbs 0 g
- Fiber 0 g
- Sugar 0 g
- Protein 28.9 g

Spicy Beef Chuck Roast

Preparation Time: 10 minutes
Cooking Time: 45 minutes
Servings: 6

Ingredients:

- 1 tablespoon olive oil
- 1 tablespoon smoked paprika
- 1 teaspoon ground cumin
- ½ teaspoon garlic powder
- ½ teaspoon onion powder
- Salt and ground black pepper, as required
- 1 (2-pound) beef chuck roast

Method:

1. In a bowl, add the oil, spices, salt and black pepper and mix well.
2. Coat the beef roast with herb mixture generously.
3. Arrange the beef roast onto the greased baking pan.
4. Select "Air Fry" of Kalorik Digital Air Fryer Oven and then adjust the temperature to 360 degrees F.
5. Set the timer for 45 minutes and press "Start/Stop" to begin cooking.
6. When the unit beeps to show that it is preheated, insert the baking pan in the Kalorik Oven.
7. When cooking time is complete, remove the sirloin roast from Kalorik Oven and place onto a cutting board.
8. With a piece of foil, cover the beef roast for about 20 minutes before slicing.
9. With a sharp knife, cut the beef roast into desired size slices and serve.

Nutritional Information per Serving:

- Calories 353
- Total Fat 15.1 g
- Saturated Fat 4.9 g
- Cholesterol 153 mg
- Sodium 128 mg
- Total Carbs 1.1 g
- Fiber 0.5 g
- Sugar 0.3 g
- Protein 50.2 g

Seasoned Beef Tenderloin

Preparation Time: 10 minutes
Cooking Time: 50 minutes
Servings: 10

Ingredients:

- 1 (3½-pound) beef tenderloin, trimmed
- 2 tablespoons olive oil
- 3 tablespoons Montreal steak seasoning

Method:

1. With kitchen twine, tie the tenderloin.
2. Rub the tenderloin with oil and season with seasoning.
3. Place the tenderloin into the greased baking pan.
4. Select "Roast" of Kalorik Digital Air Fryer Oven and then adjust the temperature to 400 degrees F.
5. Set the timer for 50 minutes and press "Start/Stop" to begin cooking.
6. When the unit beeps to show that it is preheated, insert the baking pan in the Kalorik Oven.
7. When cooking time is complete, remove the tenderloin from Kalorik Oven and place onto a cutting board for about 10 minutes before slicing.
8. With a sharp knife, cut the tenderloin into desired sized slices and serve.

Nutritional Information per Serving:

- Calories 357
- Total Fat 17.3 g
- Saturated Fat 5.9 g
- Cholesterol 146 mg
- Sodium 766 mg
- Total Carbs 0 g
- Fiber 0 g
- Sugar 0 g
- Protein 46 g

Spicy Beef Top Roast

Preparation Time: 10 minutes
Cooking Time: 45 minutes
Servings: 10

Ingredients:

- 1 tablespoon butter, melted
- 1 tablespoon balsamic vinegar
- ½ teaspoon ground cumin
- ½ teaspoon smoked paprika
- ½ teaspoon red pepper flakes, crushed
- Salt and ground black pepper, as required
- 3 pounds beef top roast

Method:

1. In a bowl, add butter, vinegar, spices, salt and black pepper and mix well.
2. Coat the roast with spice mixture generously.
3. With kitchen twines, tie the roast to keep it compact.
4. Arrange the roast onto the steak tray.
5. Select "Air Fry" of Kalorik Digital Air Fryer Oven and then adjust the temperature to 360 degrees F.
6. Set the timer for 45 minutes and press "Start/Stop" to begin cooking.
7. When the unit beeps to show that it is preheated, insert the steak tray in the Kalorik Oven.
8. When cooking time is complete, remove the roast from Kalorik Oven and place onto a cutting board for about 10 minutes before slicing.
9. With a sharp knife, cut the roast into desired sized slices and serve.

Nutritional Information per Serving:

- Calories 301
- Total Fat 20.5 g
- Saturated Fat 9.2 g
- Cholesterol 75 mg
- Sodium 96 mg
- Total Carbs 0.2 g
- Fiber 0.1 g
- Sugar 0 g
- Protein 27.8 g

Chapter 6: Lamb Recipes

Nut-Crusted Rack of Lamb

Preparation Time: 15 minutes
Cooking Time: 19 minutes
Servings: 4

Ingredients:

- 1 rack of lamb, trimmed and frenched
- Salt and ground black pepper, as required
- 1/3 cup walnuts, chopped finely
- 2 tablespoons seasoned breadcrumbs
- 2 teaspoons fresh rosemary, chopped finely
- 1 tablespoon butter, melted
- 1 tablespoon Dijon mustard

Method:

1. Insert the rotisserie rod through the rack on the meaty side of the ribs, right next to the bone.
2. Insert the rotisserie forks, one on each side of the rod to secure the rack.
3. Season the rack with salt and black pepper evenly.
4. Arrange the bacon tray in the bottom of Kalorik Digital Air Fryer Oven.
5. Select "Bake" of Kalorik Digital Air Fryer Oven and then adjust the temperature to 380 degrees F.
6. Set the timer for 12 minutes and press "Start/Stop" to begin cooking.
7. When the unit beeps to show that it is preheated, press the red lever down and load the left side of the rod into the Kalorik Oven.
8. Now, slide the rod's left side into the groove along the metal bar so it doesn't move.
9. Meanwhile, in a small bowl, mix together the remaining ingredients except the mustard.
10. When cooking time is complete, press the red lever to release the rod.
11. Remove the rack from Kalorik Oven and brush the meaty side with the mustard.
12. Then, coat the walnut mixture on all sides of the rack and press firmly.
13. Now, place the rack of lamb onto the steak tray, meat side up.
14. Select "Air Fry" and adjust the temperature to 380 degrees F.
15. Set the timer for 7 minutes and press and press "Start/Stop" to begin cooking.

16. When cooking time is complete, remove the rack of lamb from Kalorik Oven and place the rack onto a cutting board for at least 10 minutes.
17. Cut the rack into individual ribs and serve.

Nutritional Information per Serving:

- Calories 442
- Total Fat 27.3 g
- Saturated Fat 8.4 g
- Cholesterol 139 mg
- Sodium 288 mg
- Total Carbs 3.8 g
- Fiber 1.2 g
- Sugar 0.1 g
- Protein 43.5 g

Herbed Lamb Loin Chops

Preparation Time: 15 minutes
Cooking Time: 12 minutes
Servings: 2

Ingredients:

- 4 (4-ounce) (½-inch thick) lamb loin chops
- 1 teaspoon fresh thyme, minced
- 1 teaspoon fresh rosemary, minced
- 1 teaspoon fresh oregano, minced
- 2 garlic cloves, crushed
- Salt and ground black pepper, as required

Method:

1. In a large bowl, place all ingredients and mix well.
2. Refrigerate to marinate overnight.
3. Arrange the chops onto the greased steak tray.
4. Select "Bake" of Kalorik Digital Air Fryer Oven and then adjust the temperature to 400 degrees F.
5. Set the timer for 12 minutes and press "Start/Stop" to begin cooking.
6. When the unit beeps to show that it is preheated, insert the steak tray in the Kalorik Oven.
7. Flip the chops once halfway through.
8. When cooking time is complete, remove the chops from Kalorik Oven and serve hot.

Nutritional Information per Serving:

- Calories 432
- Total Fat 16.9 g
- Saturated Fat 6 g
- Cholesterol 204 mg
- Sodium 251 mg
- Total Carbs 2.2 g
- Fiber 0.8 g
- Sugar 0.1 g
- Protein 64 g

Cheesy Lamb Burgers

Preparation Time: 15 minutes
Cooking Time: 18 minutes
Servings: 4

Ingredients:

For Burgers:

- 1 pound ground lamb
- ½ cup simple breadcrumbs
- ¼ cup red onion, chopped finely
- 3 tablespoons brown mustard
- 3 teaspoons low-sodium soy sauce
- 2 teaspoons fresh parsley, chopped finely
- Salt, to taste

For Topping:

- 2 tablespoons mustard
- 1 tablespoon brown sugar
- 1 teaspoon low-sodium soy sauce
- 4 Swiss cheese slices

Method:

1. For burgers: in a large bowl, add all the ingredients and mix until well combined.
2. Make 4 equal-sized patties from the mixture.
3. Arrange the patties onto the greased steak tray in a single layer.
4. Select "Air Fry" of Kalorik Digital Air Fryer Oven and then adjust the temperature to 370 degrees F.
5. Set the timer for 15 minutes and press "Start/Stop" to begin cooking.
6. When the unit beeps to show that it is preheated, insert the steak tray in the Kalorik Oven.
7. Flip the burgers once halfway through.
8. Meanwhile, in a small bowl, add the mustard, brown sugar and soy sauce and mix well.
9. When cooking time is complete, remove the tray from Kalorik Oven and coat the burgers with mustard mixture.
10. Arrange 1 cheese slice over each burger.

11. Return the tray to the Kalorik Oven and select "Broil".
12. Set the timer for 3 minutes and press "Start/Stop".
13. When cooking time is complete, remove the burgers from Kalorik Oven and serve hot.

Nutritional Information per Serving:

- Calories 411
- Total Fat 18.5 g
- Saturated Fat 8.3 g
- Cholesterol 128 mg
- Sodium 560 mg
- Total Carbs 17.1 g
- Fiber 1.6 g
- Sugar 4.3 g
- Protein 43 g

Glazed Lamb Meatballs

Preparation Time: 20 minutes
Cooking Time: 30 minutes
Servings: 4

Ingredients:

For Meatballs:

- 1 pound ground lamb
- 10½ tablespoons quick-cooking oats
- ¼ cup Ritz crackers, crushed
- 2½ ounces evaporated milk
- 1 large egg, beaten lightly
- ½ teaspoon maple syrup
- ½ tablespoon dried onion, minced
- ½ teaspoon ground cumin
- Salt and ground black pepper, as required

For Sauce:

- 4 tablespoons orange marmalade
- 3 tablespoons maple syrup
- 2 tablespoons brown sugar
- 1 tablespoon arrowroot starch
- 1 tablespoon low-sodium soy sauce
- ½ tablespoon Worcestershire sauce
- ¼ teaspoon red pepper flakes, crushed

Method:

1. For meatballs: in a large bowl, add all the ingredients and mix until well combined.
2. Make 1½-inch balls from the mixture.
3. Arrange the meatballs into the baking pan in a single layer.
4. Select "Air Fry" of Kalorik Digital Air Fryer Oven and then adjust the temperature to 380 degrees F.
5. Set the timer for 15 minutes and press "Start/Stop" to begin cooking.
6. When the unit beeps to show that it is preheated, insert the steak tray in the Kalorik Oven.
7. Flip the meatballs once halfway through.

8. Meanwhile, for sauce: in a small pan, add all the ingredients over medium heat and cook until thickened, stirring continuously.
9. When cooking time is complete, remove the meatballs from Kalorik Oven and place onto a platter.
10. Top with sauce and serve hot.

Nutritional Information per Serving:

- Calories 440
- Total Fat 12.9 g
- Saturated Fat 4.5 g
- Cholesterol 154 mg
- Sodium 450 mg
- Total Carbs 43.8 g
- Fiber 1.7 g
- Sugar 28.1 g
- Protein 37.1 g

Maple Glazed Lamb Chops

Preparation Time: 10 minutes
Cooking Time: 15 minutes
Servings: 2

Ingredients:

- 1 tablespoon Dijon mustard
- ½ tablespoon fresh lemon juice
- 1 teaspoon maple syrup
- 1 teaspoon canola oil
- ¼ teaspoon red pepper flakes, crushed
- Salt and ground black pepper, as required
- 4 (4-ounce) lamb loin chops

Method:

1. In a black pepper large bowl, mix together the mustard, lemon juice, oil, maple syrup, red pepper flakes, salt and black pepper.
2. Add the chops and coat with the mixture generously.
3. Place the chops onto the greased steak tray.
4. Select "Bake" of Kalorik Digital Air Fryer Oven and then adjust the temperature to 390 degrees F.
5. Set the timer for 15 minutes and press "Start/Stop" to begin cooking.
6. When the unit beeps to show that it is preheated, insert the steak tray in the Kalorik Oven.
7. Flip the chops once halfway through.
8. When cooking time is complete, remove the chops from Kalorik Oven and serve hot.

Nutritional Information per Serving:

- Calories 458
- Total Fat 19.3 g
- Saturated Fat 6.2 g
- Cholesterol 204 mg
- Sodium 340 mg
- Total Carbs 2.9 g
- Fiber 0.3 g
- Sugar 2.2 g
- Protein 64.1 g

Mustard Lamb Chops

Preparation Time: 15 minutes
Cooking Time: 15 minutes
Servings: 2

Ingredients:

- 1 tablespoon Dijon mustard
- ½ tablespoon white wine vinegar
- 1 teaspoon olive oil
- ½ teaspoon dried tarragon
- Salt and ground black pepper, as required
- 4 (4-ounce) lamb loin chops

Method:

1. In a large bowl, mix together the mustard, vinegar, oil, tarragon, salt, and black pepper.
2. Add the chops and coat with the mixture generously.
3. Arrange the chops onto the greased steak tray.
4. Select "Bake" of Kalorik Digital Air Fryer Oven and then adjust the temperature to 390 degrees F.
5. Set the timer for 15 minutes and press "Start/Stop" to begin cooking.
6. When the unit beeps to show that it is preheated, insert the steak tray in the Kalorik Oven.
7. Flip the chops once halfway through.
8. When cooking time is complete, remove the chops from Kalorik Oven and serve hot.

Nutritional Information per Serving:

- Calories 448
- Total Fat 19.3 g
- Saturated Fat 6.3 g
- Cholesterol 204 mg
- Sodium 339 mg
- Total Carbs 0.5 g
- Fiber 0.3 g
- Sugar 0.1 g
- Protein 64.1 g

Herbed Leg of Lamb

Preparation Time: 15 minutes
Cooking Time: 1¼ hours
Servings: 8

Ingredients:

- 1 (2¼-pound) boneless leg of lamb
- 3 tablespoons olive oil
- Salt and ground black pepper, as required
- 2 fresh rosemary sprigs
- 2 fresh thyme sprigs

Method:

1. Rub the leg of lamb with oil and sprinkle with salt and black pepper.
2. Wrap the leg of lamb with herb sprigs.
3. Arrange the leg of lamb into the greased air frying basket.
4. Select "Air Fry" of Kalorik Digital Air Fryer Oven and then adjust the temperature to 300 degrees F.
5. Set the timer for 75 minutes and press "Start/Stop" to begin cooking.
6. When the unit beeps to show that it is preheated, insert the basket in the Kalorik Oven.
7. When cooking time is complete, remove the leg of lamb from Kalorik Oven and place onto a cutting board for about 10 minutes before slicing.
8. Cut the leg of lamb into desired sized pieces and serve.

Nutritional Information per Serving:

- Calories 285
- Total Fat 14.7 g
- Saturated Fat 4.2 g
- Cholesterol 115 mg
- Sodium 117 mg
- Total Carbs 0.5 g
- Fiber 0.4 g
- Sugar 0 g
- Protein 35.9 g

Spicy Lamb Burgers

Preparation Time: 15 minutes
Cooking Time: 10 minutes
Servings: 6

Ingredients:

- 2 pounds ground lamb
- ½ tablespoon garlic powder
- ¼ teaspoon ground cumin
- ¼ teaspoon cayenne pepper
- Salt and ground black pepper, as required

Method:

1. In a bowl, add all the ingredients and mix well.
2. Make 6 equal-sized patties from the mixture.
3. Arrange the patties onto the greased steak tray in a single layer.
4. Select "Air Fry" of Kalorik Digital Air Fryer Oven and then adjust the temperature to 360 degrees F.
5. Set the timer for 10 minutes and press "Start/Stop" to begin cooking.
6. When the unit beeps to show that it is preheated, insert the steak tray in the Kalorik Oven.
7. Flip the burgers once halfway through.
8. When cooking time is complete, remove the burgers from Kalorik Oven and serve hot.

Nutritional Information per Serving:

- Calories 284
- Total Fat 11.1 g
- Saturated Fat 4 g
- Cholesterol 136 mg
- Sodium 142 mg
- Total Carbs 0.6 g
- Fiber 0.1 g
- Sugar 0.2 g
- Protein 42.6 g

Chapter 7: Pork Recipes

Herbed Pork Chops

Preparation Time: 15 minutes
Cooking Time: 12 minutes
Servings: 4

Ingredients:

- 2 garlic cloves, minced
- ½ tablespoon fresh rosemary, chopped
- ½ tablespoon fresh parsley, chopped
- 2 tablespoons olive oil
- ¾ tablespoon Dijon mustard
- 1 tablespoon ground cumin
- 1 teaspoon sugar
- Salt and ground black pepper, as required
- 4 (6-ounces) (1-inch thick) pork chops

Method:

1. In a bowl, mix together the garlic, herbs, oil, mustard, cumin, sugar, and salt.
2. Add the pork chops and generously coat with marinade.
3. Cover the bowl and refrigerate for about 2-3 hours.
4. Remove the chops from the refrigerator and set aside at room temperature for about 30 minutes.
5. Arrange the chops onto the greased steak tray.
6. Select "Air Fry" of Kalorik Digital Air Fryer Oven and then adjust the temperature to 390 degrees F.
7. Set the timer for 12 minutes and press "Start/Stop" to begin cooking.
8. When the unit beeps to show that it is preheated, insert the steak tray in the Kalorik Oven.
9. Flip the chops once halfway through.
10. When cooking time is complete, remove the chops from Kalorik Oven and serve hot.

Nutritional Information per Serving:

- Calories 323
- Total Fat 21.5 g

- Saturated Fat 6.5 g
- Cholesterol 97 mg
- Sodium 515 mg
- Total Carbs 3 g
- Fiber 0.5 g
- Sugar 1.1 g
- Protein 32.5 g

Seasoned Pork Shoulder

Preparation Time: 15 minutes
Cooking Time: 55 minutes
Servings: 6

Ingredients:

- 2 pounds skin-on pork shoulder
- 4 tablespoons BBQ pork seasoning

Method:

1. Arrange the pork shoulder onto a cutting board, skin-side down.
2. Season the inner side of pork shoulder with seasoning.
3. With kitchen twines, tie the pork shoulder into a long round cylinder shape.
4. Season the outer side of pork shoulder with seasoning.
5. Insert the rotisserie rod through the pork shoulder.
6. Insert the rotisserie forks, one on each side of the rod to secure the pork shoulder.
7. Arrange the bacon tray in the bottom of Kalorik Digital Air Fryer Oven.
8. Select "Roast" of Kalorik Digital Air Fryer Oven and then adjust the temperature to 350 degrees F.
9. Set the timer for 55 minutes and press "Start/Stop" to begin cooking.
10. When the unit beeps to show that it is preheated, press the red lever down and load the left side of the rod into the Kalorik Oven.
11. Now, slide the rod's left side into the groove along the metal bar so it doesn't move.
12. When cooking time is complete, press the red lever to release the rod.
13. Remove the pork shoulder from Kalorik Oven and place onto a cutting board for about 10 minutes before slicing.
14. With a sharp knife, cut the pork shoulder into desired sized slices and serve.

Nutritional Information per Serving:

- Calories 448
- Total Fat 32.3 g
- Saturated Fat 11.9 g
- Cholesterol 136 mg
- Sodium 290 mg
- Total Carbs 0.7 g
- Fiber 0 g
- Sugar 0 g
- Protein 35.2 g

Simple Pork Chops

Preparation Time: 10 minutes
Cooking Time: 12 minutes
Servings: 4

Ingredients:

- 4 (6-ounce) boneless pork chops
- 1 tablespoon olive oil
- Salt and ground black pepper, as required

Method:

1. Coat both sides of the pork chops with the oil and then, rub with the salt and black pepper.
2. Place the pork chops onto the lightly greased steak tray.
3. Select "Air Fry" of Kalorik Digital Air Fryer Oven and then adjust the temperature to 400 degrees F.
4. Set the timer for 12 minutes and press "Start/Stop" to begin cooking.
5. When the unit beeps to show that it is preheated, insert the steak tray in the Kalorik Oven.
6. Flip the chops once halfway through.
7. When cooking time is complete, remove the chops from Kalorik Oven and serve hot.

Nutritional Information per Serving:

- Calories 273
- Total Fat 9.5 g
- Saturated Fat 2.5 g
- Cholesterol 124 mg
- Sodium 136 mg
- Total Carbs 0 g
- Fiber 0 g
- Sugar 0 g
- Protein 44.5 g

Glazed Ham

Preparation Time: 10 minutes
Cooking Time: 40 minutes
Servings: 6

Ingredients:

- 1½ pounds 2½ ounces ham
- 1 cup whiskey
- 2 tablespoons French mustard
- 2 tablespoons honey

Method:

1. Place the ham at room temperature for about 30 minutes before cooking.
2. In a bowl, mix together the whiskey, mustard, and honey.
3. Place the ham into the greased baking pan and coat with half of the honey mixture.
4. Select "Air Fry" of Kalorik Digital Air Fryer Oven and then adjust the temperature to 320 degrees F.
5. Set the timer for 40 minutes and press "Start/Stop" to begin cooking.
6. When the unit beeps to show that it is preheated, insert the baking pan in the Kalorik Oven.
7. After 25 minutes of cooking, turn the ham and top with the remaining honey mixture.
8. When cooking time is complete, remove the ham from Kalorik Oven and place onto a platter for about 10 minutes before slicing.
9. Cut the ham into desired size slices and serve.

Nutritional Information per Serving:

- Calories 318
- Total Fat 10.8 g
- Saturated Fat 3.7 g
- Cholesterol 71 mg
- Sodium 1600 mg
- Total Carbs 10.6 g
- Fiber 1.6 g
- Sugar 5.8 g
- Protein 20.8 g

Spicy Pork Tenderloin

Preparation Time: 10 minutes
Cooking Time: 45 minutes
Servings: 5

Ingredients:

- 1 teaspoon ground cumin
- 1 teaspoon cayenne pepper
- 1 teaspoon garlic powder
- Salt and ground black pepper, as required
- 1½ pounds pork tenderloin

Method:

1. In a bowl, mix together spices, salt and black.
2. Rub the pork with spice mixture generously.
3. Insert the rotisserie rod through the pork tenderloin.
4. Insert the rotisserie forks, one on each side of the rod to secure the pork tenderloin.
5. Insert the rotisserie forks, one on each side of the rod to secure the pork shoulder.
6. Arrange the bacon tray in the bottom of Kalorik Digital Air Fryer Oven.
7. Select "Roast" of Kalorik Digital Air Fryer Oven and then adjust the temperature to 360 degrees F.
8. Set the timer for 45 minutes and press "Start/Stop" to begin cooking.
9. When the unit beeps to show that it is preheated, press the red lever down and load the left side of the rod into the Kalorik Oven.
10. Now, slide the rod's left side into the groove along the metal bar so it doesn't move.
11. When cooking time is complete, press the red lever to release the rod.
12. Remove the pork tenderloin from Kalorik Oven and place onto a cutting board for about 10 minutes before slicing.
13. With a sharp knife, cut the pork tenderloin into desired sized slices and serve.

Nutritional Information per Serving:

- Calories 199
- Total Fat 4.9 g
- Saturated Fat 1.7 g
- Cholesterol 99 mg
- Sodium 110 mg
- Total Carbs 0.8 g
- Fiber 0.2 g
- Sugar 0.2 g
- Protein 35.8 g

Simple Pork Loin

Preparation Time: 10 minutes
Cooking Time: 30 minutes
Servings: 6

Ingredients:

- 2 pounds pork loin
- 2 tablespoons butter, melted
- Salt and ground black pepper, as required

Method:

1. Coat the pork loin with butter and then, rub with salt and black pepper generously.
2. Arrange an air rack in the baking pan.
3. Place the pork loin into the prepared baking pan.
4. Select "Air Fry" of Kalorik Digital Air Fryer Oven and then adjust the temperature to 350 degrees F.
5. Set the timer for 30 minutes and press "Start/Stop" to begin cooking.
6. When the unit beeps to show that it is preheated, insert the pan in the Kalorik Oven.
7. When cooking time is complete, remove the pork loin from Kalorik Oven and place onto a cutting board for about 10 minutes before slicing.
8. With a sharp knife, cut the pork loin into desired sized slices and serve.

Nutritional Information per Serving:

- Calories 400
- Total Fat 24.9 g
- Saturated Fat 10.3g
- Cholesterol 131 mg
- Sodium 148 mg
- Total Carbs 0 g
- Fiber 0 g
- Sugar 0 g
- Protein 41.4 g

Pork Taco Casserole

Preparation Time: 10 minutes
Cooking Time: 25 minutes
Servings: 6

Ingredients:

- 2 pounds ground pork
- 2 tablespoons taco seasoning
- 1 cup cheddar cheese, shredded
- 1 cup cottage cheese
- 1 cup salsa

Method:

1. In a bowl, add the beef and taco seasoning and mix well.
2. Add the cheeses and salsa and stir to combine.
3. Place the mixture into the baking pan.
4. Select "Air Fry" of Kalorik Digital Air Fryer Oven and then adjust the temperature to 370 degrees F.
5. Set the timer for 25 minutes and press "Start/Stop" to begin cooking.
6. When the unit beeps to show that it is preheated, insert the baking pan in the Kalorik Oven.
7. When cooking time is complete, remove the baking pan from Kalorik Oven and set aside for about 5 minutes before serving.
8. Divide the casserole into desired-sized pieces and serve.

Nutritional Information per Serving:

- Calories 348
- Total Fat 12.4 g
- Saturated Fat 6.3 g
- Cholesterol 133 mg
- Sodium 826 mg
- Total Carbs 6.3 g
- Fiber 0.7 g
- Sugar 2.1 g
- Protein 50.1 g

Honey Glazed Pork Tenderloin

Preparation Time: 15 minutes
Cooking Time: 20 minutes
Servings: 3

Ingredients:

- 2 tablespoons Sriracha
- 2 tablespoons honey
- ¼ teaspoon red pepper flakes, crushed
- Salt, as required
- 1 pound pork tenderloin

Method:

1. In a small bowl, add the Sriracha, honey, red pepper flakes and salt and mix well.
2. Brush the pork tenderloin with mixture evenly.
3. Arrange the pork tenderloin into the greased air frying basket.
4. Select "Air Fry" of Kalorik Digital Air Fryer Oven and then adjust the temperature to 350 degrees F.
5. Set the timer for 20 minutes and press "Start/Stop" to begin cooking.
6. When the unit beeps to show that it is preheated, insert the basket in the Kalorik Oven.
7. When cooking time is complete, remove the pork tenderloin from Kalorik Oven and place onto a cutting board for about 10 minutes before slicing.
8. With a sharp knife, cut the pork tenderloin into desired sized slices and serve.

Nutritional Information per Serving:

- Calories 269
- Total Fat 5.3 g
- Saturated Fat 1.8 g
- Cholesterol 110 mg
- Sodium 207 mg
- Total Carbs 13.6 g
- Fiber 0.1 g
- Sugar 39.6 g
- Protein 39.6 g

Chapter 8: Poultry Recipes

Stuffed Roasted Chicken

Preparation Time: 10 minutes
Cooking Time: 40 minutes
Servings: 6

Ingredients:

- 1 (3-pound) whole chicken, neck and giblets removed
- 1 lemon, quartered
- 3 garlic cloves, halved
- 2 fresh rosemary sprigs
- 2 tablespoons olive oil
- Salt and ground black pepper, as required

Method:

1. Stuff the chicken cavity with lemon, garlic, and rosemary sprigs.
2. With kitchen twine, tie the chicken.
3. Coat the chicken with oil evenly and then, rub with salt and black pepper.
4. Insert the rotisserie rod through the chicken.
5. Insert the rotisserie forks, one on each side of the rod to secure the rod to the chicken.
6. Arrange the bacon tray in the bottom of Kalorik Digital Air Fryer Oven.
7. Select "Roast" of Kalorik Digital Air Fryer Oven and then adjust the temperature to 375 degrees F.
8. Set the timer for 40 minutes and press "Start/Stop" to begin cooking.
9. When the unit beeps to show that it is preheated, press the red lever down and load the left side of the rod into the Kalorik Oven.
10. Now, slide the rod's left side into the groove along the metal bar so it doesn't move.
11. When cooking time is complete, press the red lever to release the rod.
12. When cooking time is complete, remove the chicken from Kalorik Oven and place onto a platter for about 10 minutes before carving.
13. With a sharp knife, cut the chicken into desired sized pieces and serve.

Nutritional Information per Serving:

- Calories 475
- Total Fat 21.6 g
- Saturated Fat 5.3 g
- Cholesterol 202 mg

- Sodium 223 mg
- Total Carbs 1 g
- Fiber 0.3 g
- Sugar 0.1 g
- Protein 65.8 g

Crispy Chicken Breasts

Preparation Time: 15 minutes
Cooking Time: 12 minutes
Servings: 6

Ingredients:

- 1 cup panko breadcrumbs
- ½ cup Parmesan cheese, grated
- ¼ cup fresh rosemary, minced
- ¼ teaspoon cayenne pepper
- Salt and ground black pepper, as required
- 6 (4-ounce) boneless, skinless chicken breasts
- 3 tablespoons olive oil
- Olive oil cooking spray

Method:

1. In a shallow dish, add the breadcrumbs, Parmesan cheese, rosemary, cayenne pepper, salt and black pepper and mix well.
2. Rub the chicken breasts with oil and then, coat with the breadcrumbs mixture evenly.
3. Arrange the chicken breasts onto the steak tray and spray with cooking spray.
4. Select "Air Fry" of Kalorik Digital Air Fryer Oven and then adjust the temperature to 350 degrees F.
5. Set the timer for 12 minutes and press "Start/Stop" to begin cooking.
6. When the unit beeps to show that it is preheated, insert the steak tray in the Kalorik Oven.
7. Flip the chicken breasts once halfway through.
8. When cooking time is complete, remove the chicken breasts from Kalorik Oven and serve hot.

Nutritional Information per Serving:

- Calories 373
- Total Fat 18.6 g
- Saturated Fat 4.8 g
- Cholesterol 106 mg
- Sodium 183 mg
- Total Carbs 4.3 g
- Fiber 1.1 g
- Sugar 0 g
- Protein 36.1 g

Herbed Cornish Hen

Preparation Time: 15 minutes
Cooking Time: 20 minutes
Servings: 2

Ingredients:

- ¼ cup olive oil
- 1 teaspoon fresh rosemary, chopped
- 1 teaspoon fresh thyme, chopped
- 1 teaspoon fresh lemon zest, grated
- ¼ teaspoon red pepper flakes, crushed
- Salt and ground black pepper, as required
- 1½ pounds Cornish game hen, backbone removed and halved

Method:

1. In a bowl, mix together oil, herbs, lemon zest and spices.
2. Add the hen portions and coat with the marinade generously.
3. Cover the bowl and refrigerate for about 24 hours.
4. In a strainer, place the hen portions and set aside to drain any liquid.
5. Arrange the bacon tray in the bottom of Kalorik Digital Air Fryer Oven.
6. Arrange the hen portions onto the greased air rack.
7. Select "Air Fry" of Kalorik Digital Air Fryer Oven and then adjust the temperature to 390 degrees F.
8. Set the timer for 20 minutes and press "Start/Stop" to begin cooking.
9. When the unit beeps to show that it is preheated, insert the air rack in the Kalorik Oven.
10. When cooking time is complete, remove the hen portions from Kalorik Oven and place onto a platter for about 10 minutes before serving.

Nutritional Information per Serving:

- Calories 828
- Total Fat 67.9 g
- Saturated Fat 15.8 g
- Cholesterol 395 mg
- Sodium 276 mg
- Total Carbs 1 g
- Fiber 0.6 g
- Sugar 0.1 g
- Protein 57.8 g

Beer Coated Duck Breast

Preparation Time: 15 minutes
Cooking Time: 20 minutes
Servings: 2

Ingredients:

- 1 cup beer
- 1 tablespoon olive oil
- 1 teaspoon mustard
- 1 tablespoon fresh thyme, chopped
- Salt and ground black pepper, as required
- 1 (10½-ounce) duck breast

Method:

1. In a bowl, add the beer, oil, mustard, thyme, salt, and black pepper and mix well
2. Add the duck breast and coat with marinade generously.
3. Cover the bowl and refrigerate for about 4 hours.
4. Arrange the duck breast onto the greased steak tray.
5. Select "Air Fry" of Kalorik Digital Air Fryer Oven and then adjust the temperature to 390 degrees F.
6. Set the timer for 20 minutes and press "Start/Stop" to begin cooking.
7. When the unit beeps to show that it is preheated, insert the steak tray in the Kalorik Oven.
8. When cooking time is complete, remove the turkey breast from Kalorik Oven and place onto a cutting board.
9. With a piece of foil, cover the duck breast for about 20 minutes before slicing.
10. With a sharp knife, cut the duck breast into desired-sized slices and serve.

Nutritional Information per Serving:

- Calories 315
- Total Fat 13.5 g
- Saturated Fat 1.1 g
- Cholesterol 0 mg
- Sodium 83 mg
- Total Carbs 5.7 g
- Fiber 0.7 g
- Sugar 0.1 g
- Protein 33.8 g

Spicy Roasted Chicken

Preparation Time: 15 minutes
Cooking Time: 1 hour 10 minutes
Servings: 6

Ingredients:

- ¼ cup butter, softened
- 2 teaspoons dried rosemary, crushed
- 1 tablespoon ground cumin
- 1 tablespoon paprika
- 1 teaspoon cayenne pepper
- 1 teaspoon garlic powder
- 1 teaspoon onion powder
- Salt and ground black pepper, as required
- 1 (3-pound) whole chicken, neck and giblets removed

Method:

1. In a bowl, add the butter, rosemary, spices, salt and black pepper mix well.
2. Rub the chicken with spice mixture generously.
3. With kitchen twine, tie off wings and legs.
4. Arrange the chicken onto the greased baking pan.
5. Select "Air Fry" of Kalorik Digital Air Fryer Oven and then adjust the temperature to 370 degrees F.
6. Set the timer for 70 minutes and press "Start/Stop" to begin cooking.
7. When the unit beeps to show that it is preheated, insert the baking pan in the Kalorik Oven.
8. When cooking time is complete, remove the chicken from Kalorik Oven and place onto a platter for about 10 minutes before carving.
9. With a sharp knife, cut the chicken into desired sized pieces and serve.

Nutritional Information per Serving:

- Calories 511
- Total Fat 25 g
- Saturated Fat 9.6 g
- Cholesterol 222 mg
- Sodium 279 mg
- Total Carbs 2.2 g
- Fiber 0.9 g
- Sugar 0.4 g
- Protein 66.2 g

Buttered Turkey Breast

Preparation Time: 15 minutes
Cooking Time: 55 minutes
Servings: 6

Ingredients:

- ¼ cup butter, softened
- 4 tablespoons fresh rosemary, chopped
- Salt and ground black pepper, as required
- 1 (4-pound) bone-in, skin-on turkey breast
- 2 tablespoons olive oil

Method:

1. In a bowl, add the butter, rosemary, salt and black pepper and mix well.
2. Rub the herb mixture under skin evenly.
3. Coat the outside of turkey breast with oil.
4. Place the turkey breast into the greased baking pan.
5. Select "Bake" of Kalorik Digital Air Fryer Oven and then adjust the temperature to 350 degrees F.
6. Set the timer for 55 minutes and press "Start/Stop" to begin cooking.
7. When the unit beeps to show that it is preheated, insert the baking pan in the Kalorik Oven.
8. When cooking time is complete, remove the turkey breast from Kalorik Oven and place onto a cutting board.
9. With a piece of foil, cover the turkey breast for about 20 minutes before slicing.
10. With a sharp knife, cut the turkey breast into desired-sized slices and serve.

Nutritional Information per Serving:

- Calories 628
- Total Fat 34.3 g
- Saturated Fat 11.1 g
- Cholesterol 209 mg
- Sodium 461 mg
- Total Carbs 1.4 g
- Fiber 0.9 g
- Sugar 0 g
- Protein 65 g

Garlicky Duck Legs

Preparation Time: 10 minutes
Cooking Time: 30 minutes
Servings: 2

Ingredients:

- 2 garlic cloves, minced
- 1 tablespoon fresh parsley, chopped
- 1 teaspoon five-spice powder
- Salt and ground black pepper, as required
- 2 duck legs

Method:

1. In a bowl, mix add the garlic, parsley, five-spice powder, salt and black pepper and mix until well combined.
2. Rub the duck legs with garlic mixture generously.
3. Arrange the duck legs onto the greased steak tray.
4. Select "Air Fry" of Kalorik Digital Air Fryer Oven and then adjust the temperature to 340 degrees F.
5. Set the timer for 30 minutes and press "Start/Stop" to begin cooking.
6. When the unit beeps to show that it is preheated, insert the steak tray in the Kalorik Oven.
7. When cooking time is complete, remove the turkey legs from Kalorik Oven and serve hot.

Nutritional Information per Serving:

- Calories 434
- Total Fat 14.4 g
- Saturated Fat 3.2 g
- Cholesterol 253 mg
- Sodium 339 mg
- Total Carbs 1.1 g
- Fiber 0.1 g
- Sugar 0.1 g
- Protein 70.4 g

Simple Turkey Breast

Preparation Time: 10 minutes
Cooking Time: 45 minutes
Servings: 8

Ingredients:

- 1 (3-pound) turkey breast half
- 1 tablespoon cayenne pepper
- Salt and ground black pepper, as required

Method:

1. Rub the turkey breast with the cayenne pepper, salt and black pepper evenly.
2. Arrange the turkey breast onto the greased steak tray.
3. Select "Bake" of Kalorik Digital Air Fryer Oven and then adjust the temperature to 360 degrees F.
4. Set the timer for 45 minutes and press "Start/Stop" to begin cooking.
5. When the unit beeps to show that it is preheated, insert the steak tray in the Kalorik Oven.
6. When cooking time is complete, remove the turkey breast from Kalorik Oven and place onto a cutting board.
7. With a piece of foil, cover the turkey breast for about 20 minutes before slicing.
8. With a sharp knife, cut the turkey breast into desired-sized slices and serve.

Nutritional Information per Serving:

- Calories 227
- Total Fat 10.6 g
- Saturated Fat 3 g
- Cholesterol 90 mg
- Sodium 890 mg
- Total Carbs 1.9 g
- Fiber 0.2 g
- Sugar 0.1 g
- Protein 30.1 g

Herbed Chicken Thighs

Preparation Time: 10 minutes
Cooking Time: 20 minutes
Servings: 4

Ingredients:

- ½ tablespoon fresh rosemary, minced
- ½ tablespoon fresh thyme, minced
- Salt and ground black pepper, as required
- 4 (5-ounce) chicken thighs
- 2 tablespoons olive oil

Method:

1. In a large bowl, add the herbs, salt and black pepper and mix well.
2. Coat the chicken thighs with oil and then, rub with herb mixture.
3. Arrange the chicken thighs onto the greased steak tray.
4. Select "Air Fry" of Kalorik Digital Air Fryer Oven and then adjust the temperature to 400 degrees F.
5. Set the timer for 20 minutes and press "Start/Stop" to begin cooking.
6. When the unit beeps to show that it is preheated, insert the steak tray in the Kalorik Oven.
7. Flip the chicken thighs once halfway through.
8. When cooking time is complete, remove the chicken thighs from Kalorik Oven and serve hot.

Nutritional Information per Serving:

- Calories 332
- Total Fat 17.6 g
- Saturated Fat 3.9 g
- Cholesterol 126 mg
- Sodium 161 mg
- Total Carbs 0.5 g
- Fiber 0.3 g
- Sugar 0 g
- Protein 41.1 g

Glazed Chicken Drumsticks

Preparation Time: 15 minutes
Cooking Time: 20 minutes
Servings: 4

Ingredients:

- ¼ cup Dijon mustard
- 1 tablespoon honey
- 2 tablespoons canola oil
- 1 tablespoon fresh parsley, minced
- Salt and ground black pepper, as required
- 4 (6-ounce) chicken drumsticks

Method:

1. Marinated the chicken drumsticks with all the above ingredients for overnight. Preheat Philips Airfryer at 160 degree. In bowl, add all ingredients except the drumsticks and mix until well combined.
2. Add the drumsticks and coat with the mixture generously.
3. Cover the bowl and place in the refrigerator to marinate overnight.
4. Place the chicken drumsticks into the greased baking pan.
5. Select "Air Fry" of Kalorik Digital Air Fryer Oven and then adjust the temperature to 320 degrees F.
6. Set the timer for 12 minutes and press "Start/Stop" to begin cooking.
7. When the unit beeps to show that it is preheated, insert the steak tray in the Kalorik Oven.
8. After 12 minutes, flip the drumsticks and set the temperature to 390 degrees F for 8 minutes.
9. When cooking time is complete, remove the chicken drumsticks from Kalorik Oven and serve hot.

Nutritional Information per Serving:

- Calories 376
- Total Fat 17.4 g
- Saturated Fat 3.1 g
- Cholesterol 150 mg
- Sodium 353 mg
- Total Carbs 5.2 g
- Fiber 0.6 g
- Sugar 4.5 g
- Protein 47.5 g

Chapter 9: Fish & Seafood Recipes

Trout with Broccoli

Preparation Time: 15 minutes
Cooking Time: 12 minutes
Servings: 2

Ingredients:

- 1 cup small broccoli florets
- 2 tablespoons olive oil, divided
- Salt and ground black pepper, as required
- ½ teaspoon fresh ginger, grated
- 1 tablespoon soy sauce
- 1 teaspoon fresh lime juice
- 1 teaspoon brown sugar
- ¼ teaspoon cornstarch
- 2 (6-ounce) trout fillets
- 1 scallion, thinly sliced

Method:

1. In a bowl, mix together the broccoli, 1 tablespoon of oil, salt, and black pepper.
2. In another bowl, add the ginger, soy sauce, lime juice, brown sugar, and cornstarch and mix until well combined.
3. Coat the trout fillets with remaining oil and then with the ginger mixture.
4. Arrange the broccoli florets into the greased air frying basket and top with the trout fillets.
5. Select "Air Fry" of Kalorik Digital Air Fryer Oven and then adjust the temperature to 375 degrees F.
6. Set the timer for 12 minutes and press "Start/Stop" to begin cooking.
7. When the unit beeps to show that it is preheated, insert the basket in the Kalorik Oven.
8. When cooking time is complete, remove the basket from Kalorik Oven and serve hot

Nutritional Information per Serving:

- Calories 474
- Total Fat 28.6 g

- Saturated Fat 4.5 g
- Cholesterol 126 mg
- Sodium 582 mg
- Total Carbs 6.3 g
- Fiber 1.5 g
- Sugar 2.6 g
- Protein 47.3 g

Herbed Salmon

Preparation Time: 10 minutes
Cooking Time: 12 minutes
Servings: 4

Ingredients:

- 1 tablespoon fresh parsley, minced
- 1 tablespoon fresh rosemary, minced
- Salt and ground black pepper, as required
- 4 (6-ounce) salmon fillets

Method:

1. In a small bowl, mix together herbs, salt and black pepper.
2. Rub the salmon fillets with herb mixture evenly.
3. Arrange the salmon fillets onto the greased air rack.
4. Select "Broil" of Kalorik Digital Air Fryer Oven and set the timer for 12 minutes.
5. Press "Start/Stop" to begin cooking.
6. When the unit beeps to show that it is preheated, insert the air rack in the Kalorik Oven.
7. When cooking time is complete, remove the salmon fillets from Kalorik Oven and serve hot.

Nutritional Information per Serving:

- Calories 228
- Total Fat 10.6 g
- Saturated Fat 1.6 g
- Cholesterol 75 mg
- Sodium 115 mg
- Total Carbs 0.6 g
- Fiber 0.4 g
- Sugar 0 g
- Protein 33.1 g

Tangy Sea Bass

Preparation Time: 10 minutes
Cooking Time: 12 minutes
Servings: 2

Ingredients:

- 2 (5-ounce) sea bass fillets
- 1 garlic clove, minced
- 1 teaspoon fresh dill, minced
- 1 tablespoon olive oil
- 1 tablespoon balsamic vinegar
- Salt and ground black pepper, as required

Method:

1. In a large resealable bag, add all the ingredients.
2. Seal the bag and shale well to mix.
3. Refrigerate to marinate for at least 30 minutes.
4. Remove the fish fillets from bag and shake off the excess marinade.
5. Arrange the fish fillets onto the greased steak tray in a single layer.
6. Select "Bake" of Kalorik Digital Air Fryer Oven and then adjust the temperature to 450 degrees F.
7. Set the timer for 12 minutes and press "Start/Stop" to begin cooking.
8. When the unit beeps to show that it is preheated, insert the steak tray in the Kalorik Oven.
9. Flip the fish fillets once halfway through.
10. When cooking time is complete, remove the fish fillets from Kalorik Oven and serve hot.

Nutritional Information per Serving:

- Calories 241
- Total Fat 10.7 g
- Saturated Fat 1.9 g
- Cholesterol 75 mg
- Sodium 203 mg
- Total Carbs 0.9 g
- Fiber 0.1 g
- Sugar 0.1 g
- Protein 33.7 g

Glazed Salmon

Preparation Time: 10 minutes
Cooking Time: 12 minutes
Servings: 2

Ingredients:

- 1/3 cup soy sauce
- 1/3 cup maple syrup
- 3 teaspoons fresh lemon juice
- 1 teaspoon water
- 4 (3½-ounce) salmon fillets

Method:

1. In a small bowl, mix together the soy sauce, maple syrup, lemon juice and water.
2. reserve about half of the mixture in another small bowl,
3. Add salmon fillets in the remaining mixture and coat well.
4. Cover the bowl and refrigerate to marinate for about 2 hours.
5. Remove the salmon fillets from refrigerator and arrange into the greased air frying basket.
6. Select "Air Fry" of Kalorik Digital Air Fryer Oven and then adjust the temperature to 355 degrees F.
7. Set the timer for 12 minutes and press "Start/Stop" to begin cooking.
8. When the unit beeps to show that it is preheated, insert the basket in the Kalorik Oven.
9. Flip the salmon fillets once halfway through and then, coat with the reserved marinade after every 3 minutes.
10. When cooking time is complete, remove the salmon fillets from Kalorik Oven and serve hot.

Nutritional Information per Serving:

- Calories 424
- Total Fat 12.4 g
- Saturated Fat 1.8 g
- Cholesterol 88 mg
- Sodium 1500 mg
- Total Carbs 38.6 g
- Fiber 0.4 g
- Sugar 32.1 g
- Protein 41.2 g

Cajun Spiced Salmon

Preparation Time: 10 minutes
Cooking Time: 11 minutes
Servings: 2

Ingredients:

- 2 (6-ounce) (1½-inch thick) salmon fillets
- 2 teaspoons butter, melted
- 1 tablespoon Cajun seasoning

Method:

1. Drizzle the salmon fillets with butter and then, rub with the seasoning.
2. Arrange the salmon fillets into the greased air frying basket.
3. Select "Air Fry" of Kalorik Digital Air Fryer Oven and then adjust the temperature to 390 degrees F.
4. Set the timer for 11 minutes and press "Start/Stop" to begin cooking.
5. When the unit beeps to show that it is preheated, insert the basket in the Kalorik Oven.
6. When cooking time is complete, remove the salmon fillets from Kalorik Oven and serve hot.

Nutritional Information per Serving:

- Calories 259
- Total Fat 14.3 g
- Saturated Fat 3.9 g
- Cholesterol 85 mg
- Sodium 177 mg
- Total Carbs 0 g
- Fiber 0 g
- Sugar 0 g
- Protein 33.1 g

Buttered Salmon

Preparation Time: 10 minutes
Cooking Time: 10 minutes
Servings: 2

Ingredients:

- 2 (6-ounces) salmon fillets
- Salt and ground black pepper, as required
- 1 tablespoon butter, melted

Method:

1. Season each salmon fillet with salt and black pepper and then, coat with the butter.
2. Arrange the salmon fillets onto the greased steak tray in a single layer.
3. Select "Air Fry" of Kalorik Digital Air Fryer Oven and then adjust the temperature to 360 degrees F.
4. Set the timer for 12 minutes and press "Start/Stop" to begin cooking.
5. When the unit beeps to show that it is preheated, insert the steak tray in the Kalorik Oven.
6. When cooking time is complete, remove the fish fillets from Kalorik Oven and serve hot.

Nutritional Information per Serving:

- Calories 276
- Total Fat 16.3 g
- Saturated Fat 5.2 g
- Cholesterol 90 mg
- Sodium 193 mg
- Total Carbs 0 g
- Fiber 0 g
- Sugar 0 g
- Protein 33.1 g

Shrimp Burgers

Preparation Time: 15 minutes
Cooking Time: 6 minutes
Servings: 2

Ingredients:

- ½ cup shrimp, peeled, deveined and chopped very finely
- ½ cup panko breadcrumbs
- 2 tablespoons onion, chopped finely
- ¼ teaspoon fresh ginger, minced
- ¼ teaspoon garlic, minced
- ¼ teaspoon ground cumin
- ¼ teaspoon cayenne pepper
- 1/8 teaspoon ground turmeric
- Salt and ground black pepper, as required

Method:

1. In a bowl, add all ingredients and mix until well combined.
2. Make small sized patties from mixture.
3. Arrange the patties onto the greased air fryer basket in a single layer.
4. Select "Air Fry" of Kalorik Digital Air Fryer Oven and then adjust the temperature to 355 degrees F.
5. Set the timer for 6 minutes and press "Start/Stop" to begin cooking.
6. When the unit beeps to show that it is preheated, insert the basket in the Kalorik Oven.
7. When cooking time is complete, remove the burgers from Kalorik Oven and serve hot.

Nutritional Information per Serving:

- Calories 240
- Total Fat 3.9 g
- Saturated Fat 1.4 g
- Cholesterol 239 mg
- Sodium 355 mg
- Total Carbs 7.4 g
- Fiber 0.5 g
- Sugar 0.5 g
- Protein 26.8 g

Rosemary Tilapia

Preparation Time: 15 minutes
Cooking Time: 12 minutes
Servings: 2

Ingredients:

- 2 (6-ounce) tilapia fillets
- 1 tablespoon olive oil
- 1 teaspoon fresh rosemary, minced
- Salt and ground black pepper, as require

Method:

1. Coat the tilapia fillets with oil and then rub with rosemary, salt and black pepper.
2. Arrange the tilapia fillets onto a lightly greased air rack, skin-side down.
3. Select "Air Fry" of Kalorik Digital Air Fryer Oven and then adjust the temperature to 360 degrees F.
4. Set the timer for 12 minutes and press "Start/Stop" to begin cooking.
5. When the unit beeps to show that it is preheated, insert the air rack in the Kalorik Oven.
6. When cooking time is complete, remove the fish fillets from Kalorik Oven and serve hot.

Nutritional Information per Serving:

- Calories 202
- Total Fat 8.6 g
- Saturated 1.7 g
- Cholesterol 83 mg
- Sodium 138 mg
- Total Carbs 0.4 g
- Fiber 0.3 g
- Sugar 0 g
- Protein 31.7 g

Halibut & Shrimp with Pasta

Preparation Time: 15 minutes
Cooking Time: 18 minutes
Servings: 4

Ingredients:

- 14 ounces pasta
- 4 tablespoons pesto, divided
- 4 (4-ounce) halibut steaks
- 2 tablespoons olive oil
- ½ pound tomatoes, chopped
- 8 large shrimp, peeled and deveined
- 2 tablespoons fresh lime juice
- 2 tablespoons fresh dill, chopped

Method:

1. In the bottom of a baking pan, spread 1 tablespoon of pesto.
2. Place halibut steaks and tomatoes over pesto in a single layer and drizzle with the oil.
3. Now, place the shrimp on top in a single layer.
4. Drizzle with lime juice and sprinkle with dill.
5. Select "Air Fry" of Kalorik Digital Air Fryer Oven and then adjust the temperature to 390 degrees F.
6. Set the timer for 8 minutes and press "Start/Stop" to begin cooking.
7. When the unit beeps to show that it is preheated, place the cake pan over the air rack and insert in the Kalorik Oven.
8. Meanwhile, in a large pan of salted boiling water, add the pasta and cook for about 8-10 minutes or until desired doneness.
9. Drain the pasta and transfer into a large bowl.
10. Add the remaining pesto and toss to coat well.
11. When cooking time is complete, remove the pan from Kalorik Oven.
12. Divide the pasta onto serving plate and top with fish mixture.
13. Serve immediately.

Nutritional Information per Serving:

- Calories 606
- Total Fat 19.4 g
- Saturated Fat 3.2 g
- Cholesterol 205 mg

- Sodium 294 mg
- Total Carbs 59.1 g
- Fiber 1.1 g
- Sugar 2.5 g
- Protein 47.4 g

Sweet & Sour Halibut

Preparation Time: 10 minutes
Cooking Time: 12 minutes
Servings: 4

Ingredients:

- 4 (5-ounce) halibut fillets
- 2 garlic clove, minced
- 1 tablespoon fresh dill, minced
- 2 tablespoons butter, melted
- 2 tablespoons fresh lime juice
- ½ teaspoon honey
- ¼ teaspoon Sriracha

Method:

1. In a large resealable bag, place all the ingredients and seal the bag.
2. Shake the bag well to mix.
3. Place the bag in the refrigerator to marinate for at least 30 minutes.
4. Remove the fish fillets from bag and shake off the excess marinade.
5. Arrange the halibut fillets onto the greased steak tray.
6. Select "Bake" of Kalorik Digital Air Fryer Oven and then adjust the temperature to 400 degrees F.
7. Set the timer for 12 minutes and press "Start/Stop" to begin cooking.
8. When the unit beeps to show that it is preheated, insert the steak tray in the Kalorik Oven.
9. When cooking time is complete, remove the fish fillets from Kalorik Oven and serve hot.

Nutritional Information per Serving:

- Calories 216
- Total Fat 9.1 g
- Saturated Fat 4.1 g
- Cholesterol 61 mg
- Sodium 120 mg
- Total Carbs 1.8 g
- Fiber 0.1 g
- Sugar 0.7 g
- Protein 30.2 g

Chapter 10: Vegetarian Recipes

Buttered Zucchini

Preparation Time: 15 minutes
Cooking Time: 15 minutes
Servings: 6

Ingredients:

- 2 tablespoons butter, melted
- 2 pounds zucchini, sliced
- ½ teaspoon dried rosemary, crushed
- ½ teaspoon ground cumin
- ½ teaspoon ground coriander
- ½ teaspoon cayenne pepper
- Salt and ground black pepper, as required

Method:

1. In a large bowl, add all ingredients and mix well.
2. Place the zucchini slices into the greased air fryer basket in a single layer.
3. Select "Air Fry" of Kalorik Digital Air Fryer Oven and then adjust the temperature to 390 degrees F.
4. Set the timer for 15 minutes and press "Start/Stop" to begin cooking.
5. When the unit beeps to show that it is preheated, insert the basket in the Kalorik Oven.
6. When cooking time is complete, remove the zucchini from Kalorik Oven and serve hot.

Nutritional Information per Serving:

- Calories 60
- Total Fat 4.2 g
- Saturated Fat 2.5 g
- Cholesterol 10 mg
- Sodium 70 mg
- Total Carbs 5.3 g
- Fiber 1.8 g
- Sugar 2.6 g
- Protein 1.9 g

Buttered Broccoli

Preparation Time: 10 minutes
Cooking Time: 20 minutes
Servings: 4

Ingredients:

- 3 cups broccoli, cut into 1-inch pieces
- 1 tablespoon butter, melted
- Salt, as required

Method:

1. In a bowl, add the broccoli, butter and salt and toss to coat well.
2. Arrange the broccoli pieces into the greased air fryer basket in a single layer.
3. Select "Air Fry" of Kalorik Digital Air Fryer Oven and then adjust the temperature to 375 degrees F.
4. Set the timer for 20 minutes and press "Start/Stop" to begin cooking.
5. When the unit beeps to show that it is preheated, insert the basket in the Kalorik Oven.
6. When cooking time is complete, remove the broccoli from Kalorik Oven and serve hot.

Nutritional Information per Serving:

- Calories 49
- Total Fat 3.1 g
- Saturated Fat 1.8 g
- Cholesterol 8 mg
- Sodium 82 mg
- Total Carbs 4.5 g
- Fiber 1.8 g
- Sugar 1.2 g
- Protein 1.9 g

Buttered Asparagus

Preparation Time: 10 minutes
Cooking Time: 6 minutes
Servings: 3

Ingredients:

- 1 pound asparagus, trimmed
- 2 tablespoons butter, melted
- 2 tablespoons fresh lemon juice
- Salt and ground black pepper, as required
- 3 tablespoons Parmesan cheese, shredded

Method:

1. In a bowl, mix together the asparagus, butter, lemon juice, salt, and black pepper.
2. Arrange the asparagus into the greased air fryer basket in a single layer.
3. Select "Air Fry" of Kalorik Digital Air Fryer Oven and then adjust the temperature to 400 degrees F.
4. Set the timer for 6 minutes and press "Start/Stop" to begin cooking.
5. When the unit beeps to show that it is preheated, insert the basket in the Kalorik Oven.
6. When cooking time is complete, remove the asparagus from Kalorik Oven and transfer into a bowl.
7. Stir in the Parmesan and serve hot.

Nutritional Information per Serving:

- Calories 121
- Total Fat 9.3 g
- Saturated Fat 5.9 g
- Cholesterol 24 mg
- Sodium 195 mg
- Total Carbs 6.3 g
- Fiber 3.2 g
- Sugar 3.1 g
- Protein 5.4 g

Balsamic Green Beans

Preparation Time: 15 minutes
Cooking Time: 12 minutes
Servings: 3

Ingredients:

- 1 pound green beans, trimmed
- 2 garlic cloves, minced
- 1 tablespoon vegetable oil
- 1 tablespoon balsamic vinegar
- Salt and ground black pepper, as required

Method:

1. In a large bowl, add all the ingredients and toss to coat well.
2. Arrange the green beans into the greased air fryer basket in a single layer.
3. Select "Air Fry" of Kalorik Digital Air Fryer Oven and then adjust the temperature to 400 degrees F.
4. Set the timer for 12 minutes and press "Start/Stop" to begin cooking.
5. When the unit beeps to show that it is preheated, insert the basket in the Kalorik Oven.
6. When cooking time is complete, remove the green beans from Kalorik Oven and serve hot.

Nutritional Information per Serving:

- Calories 91
- Total Fat 4.7 g
- Saturated Fat 0.9 g
- Cholesterol 0 mg
- Sodium 60 mg
- Total Carbs 11.5 g
- Fiber 5.2 g
- Sugar 2.2 g
- Protein 2.9 g

Tofu with Broccoli

Preparation Time: 15 minutes
Cooking Time: 15 minutes
Servings: 2

Ingredients:

- 7 ounces firm tofu, pressed, drained and cubed
- 1 small broccoli head, cut into florets
- 1 tablespoon olive oil
- 1 tablespoon nutritional yeast
- Salt and ground black pepper, as required

Method:

1. In a bowl, add all ingredients and toss to coat well.
2. Place the tofu mixture in the air fryer basket.
3. Select "Air Fry" of Kalorik Digital Air Fryer Oven and then adjust the temperature to 390 degrees F.
4. Set the timer for 15 minutes and press "Start/Stop" to begin cooking.
5. When the unit beeps to show that it is preheated, insert the basket in the Kalorik Oven.
6. When cooking time is complete, remove the tofu mixture from Kalorik Oven and serve hot.

Nutritional Information per Serving:

- Calories 176
- Total Fat 11.7 g
- Saturated 1.9 g
- Cholesterol 0 mg
- Sodium 120 mg
- Total Carbs 9.6 g
- Fiber 4.4 g
- Sugar 2.1 g
- Protein 12.8 g

Glazed Mushrooms

Preparation Time: 10 minutes
Cooking Time: 15 minutes
Servings: 4

Ingredients:

- ½ cup low-sodium soy sauce
- 4 tablespoons fresh lemon juice
- 1 tablespoon maple syrup
- 4 garlic cloves, finely chopped
- Ground black pepper, as required
- 20 ounces fresh cremini mushrooms, halved

Method:

1. In a bowl, add the soy sauce, lemon juice, maple syrup, garlic and black pepper and mix well. Set aside.
2. Place the mushroom into the greased baking pan in a single layer.
3. Select "Air Fry" of Kalorik Digital Air Fryer Oven and then adjust the temperature to 350 degrees F.
4. Set the timer for 15 minutes and press "Start/Stop" to begin cooking.
5. When the unit beeps to show that it is preheated, insert the baking pan in the Kalorik Oven.
6. After 10 minutes of cooking, in the pan, add the soy sauce mixture and stir to combine.
7. When cooking time is complete, remove the mushrooms from Kalorik Oven and serve hot.

Nutritional Information per Serving:

- Calories 70
- Total Fat 0.3 g
- Saturated Fat 0.1 g
- Cholesterol 0 mg
- Sodium 1600 mg
- Total Carbs 12.5 g
- Fiber 1 g
- Sugar 7.8 g
- Protein 5.9 g

Lemony Okra

Preparation Time: 10 minutes
Cooking Time: 20 minutes
Servings: 2

Ingredients:

- 1 (10-ounce) bag frozen cut okra
- ¼ cup nutritional yeast
- 2 tablespoons fresh lemon juice
- Salt and ground black pepper, as required

Method:

1. In a bowl, add the okra, nutritional yeast, lemon juice, salt, and black pepper and toss to coat well.
2. Arrange the okra into the greased air fryer basket in a single layer.
3. Select "Air Fry" of Kalorik Digital Air Fryer Oven and then adjust the temperature to 400 degrees F.
4. Set the timer for 20 minutes and press "Start/Stop" to begin cooking.
5. When the unit beeps to show that it is preheated, insert the basket in the Kalorik Oven.
6. When cooking time is complete, remove the okra from Kalorik Oven and serve hot.

Nutritional Information per Serving:

- Calories 131
- Total Fat 1.5 g
- Saturated Fat 0.3 g
- Cholesterol 0 mg
- Sodium 103 mg
- Total Carbs 20.1 g
- Fiber 9.6 g
- Sugar 2.4 g
- Protein 12.1 g

Spiced Sweet Potatoes

Preparation Time: 15 minutes
Cooking Time: 20 minutes
Servings: 4

Ingredients:

- 3 large sweet potatoes, peeled and cut in 1-inch cubes
- 2 tablespoons vegetable oil
- ½ teaspoon ground cumin
- ½ teaspoon red chili powder
- Salt and ground black pepper, as required

Method:

1. In a large bowl, add all the ingredients and toss to coat well.
2. Arrange the sweet potato cubes into the greased air fryer basket in a single layer.
3. Select "Roast" of Kalorik Digital Air Fryer Oven and then adjust the temperature to 415 degrees F.
4. Set the timer for 20 minutes and press "Start/Stop" to begin cooking.
5. When the unit beeps to show that it is preheated, insert the basket in the Kalorik Oven.
6. When cooking time is complete, remove the sweet potato cubes from Kalorik Oven and serve hot.

Nutritional Information per Serving:

- Calories 195
- Total Fat 7.1 g
- Saturated Fat 1.4 g
- Cholesterol 0 mg
- Sodium 53 mg
- Total Carbs 31.7 g
- Fiber 4.8 g
- Sugar 0.6 g
- Protein 1.8 g

Spiced Cauliflower

Preparation Time: 15 minutes
Cooking Time: 15 minutes
Servings: 3

Ingredients:

- 1 pound cauliflower head, cut into florets
- 1 tablespoon olive oil
- ½ teaspoon dried parsley, crushed
- 1 teaspoon smoked paprika
- ½ teaspoon ground cumin
- ¼ teaspoon ground turmeric
- Salt and ground black pepper, as required

Method:

1. In a bowl, add all the ingredients and toss to coat well.
2. Place the cauliflower florets in the air fryer basket.
3. Select "Air Fry" of Kalorik Digital Air Fryer Oven and then adjust the temperature to 400 degrees F.
4. Set the timer for 15 minutes and press "Start/Stop" to begin cooking.
5. When the unit beeps to show that it is preheated, insert the basket in the Kalorik Oven.
6. When cooking time is complete, remove the cauliflower florets from Kalorik Oven and serve hot.

Nutritional Information per Serving:

- Calories 82
- Total Fat 5 g
- Saturated Fat 0.71 g
- Cholesterol 0 mg
- Sodium 97 mg
- Total Carbs 8.7 g
- Fiber 4.1 g
- Sugar 3.7 g
- Protein 3.2 g

Lemony Brussels Sprout

Preparation Time: 15 minutes
Cooking Time: 20 minutes
Servings: 3

Ingredients:

- 1 pound Brussels Sprouts, trimmed and cut into bite-sized pieces
- 1 tablespoon fresh lemon juice
- 1 tablespoon butter, melted
- ½ teaspoon fresh lemon zest, grated
- Salt and ground black pepper, as required

Method:

1. In a bowl, add all the ingredients and toss to coat well.
2. Place the Brussels Sprout in the air fryer basket.
3. Select "Air Fry" of Kalorik Digital Air Fryer Oven and then adjust the temperature to 350 degrees F.
4. Set the timer for 20 minutes and press "Start/Stop" to begin cooking.
5. When the unit beeps to show that it is preheated, insert the basket in the Kalorik Oven.
6. When cooking time is complete, remove the Brussels sprout from Kalorik Oven and serve hot.

Nutritional Information per Serving:

- Calories 101
- Total Fat 4.4 g
- Saturated Fat 2.6 g
- Cholesterol 10 mg
- Sodium 116 mg
- Total Carbs 13.9 g
- Fiber 5.7 g
- Sugar 3.4 g
- Protein 5.2 g

Chapter 11: Dessert Recipes

Raspberry Danish

Preparation Time: 20 minutes
Cooking Time: 25 minutes
Servings: 6

Ingredients:

- 1 tube full-sheet crescent roll dough
- 4 ounces cream cheese, softened
- ¼ cup raspberry jam
- ½ cup fresh raspberries, chopped
- 1 cup powdered sugar
- 2-3 tablespoons heavy whipping cream

Method:

1. Place the sheet of crescent roll dough onto a flat surface and unroll it.
2. In a microwave-safe bowl, add the cream cheese and microwave for about 20-30 seconds.
3. Remove from microwave and stir until creamy and smooth.
4. Spread the cream cheese over the dough sheet, followed by the strawberry jam.
5. Now, place the raspberry pieces evenly across the top.
6. From the short side, roll the dough and pinch the seam to seal.
7. Arrange a greased parchment paper onto the steak tray of oven.
8. Carefully, curve the rolled pastry into a horseshoe shape and arrange onto the prepared tray.
9. Select "Air Fry" of Kalorik Digital Air Fryer Oven and then adjust the temperature to 350 degrees F.
10. Set the timer for 25 minutes and press "Start/Stop" to begin cooking.
11. When the unit beeps to show that it is preheated, insert the tray in the Kalorik Oven.
12. When cooking time is complete, remove the tray from Kalorik Oven and place onto a rack to cool.
13. Meanwhile, in a bowl, mix together the powdered sugar and cream.
14. Drizzle the cream mixture over cooled Danish and serve.

Nutritional Information per Serving:

- Calories 335
- Total Fat 15.3 g
- Saturated Fat 8 g
- Cholesterol 28 mg
- Sodium 342 mg
- Total Carbs 45.3 g
- Fiber 0.7 g
- Sugar 30.1 g
- Protein 4.4 g

Blueberry Muffins

Preparation Time: 15 minutes
Cooking Time: 15 minutes
Servings: 8

Ingredients:

- ¼ cup unsweetened coconut milk
- 2 large eggs
- ½ teaspoon vanilla extract
- 1½ cups almond flour
- ¼ cup Swerve
- 1 teaspoon baking powder
- ¼ teaspoon ground cinnamon
- Pinch of ground cloves
- Pinch of ground nutmeg
- 1/8 teaspoon salt
- ½ cup fresh blueberries
- ¼ cup pecans, chopped

Method:

1. In a blender, add the almond milk, eggs and vanilla extract and pulse for about 20-30 seconds.
2. Add the almond flour, Swerve, baking powder, spices and salt and pulse for about 30-45 seconds until well blended.
3. Transfer the mixture into a bowl
4. Gently, fold in half of the blueberries and pecans.
5. Place the mixture into 8 silicone muffin cups and top each with remaining blueberries.
6. Select "Air Fry" of Kalorik Digital Air Fryer Oven and then adjust the temperature to 325 degrees F.
7. Set the timer for 15 minutes and press "Start/Stop" to begin cooking.
8. When the unit beeps to show that it is preheated, place the cups over the air rack and insert in the Kalorik Oven.
9. When cooking time is complete, remove the cups from Kalorik Oven and place onto a wire rack to cool for about 10 minutes.
10. Carefully, invert the muffins onto the wire rack to completely cool before serving.

Nutritional Information per Serving:

- Calories 191
- Total Fat 16.5 g
- Saturated Fat 3 g
- Cholesterol 47 mg
- Sodium 54 mg
- Total Carbs 14.8 g
- Fiber 3.2 g
- Sugar 9.7 g
- Protein 6.8 g

Lemon Mousse

Preparation Time: 10 minutes
Cooking Time: 12 minutes
Servings: 2

Ingredients:

- 4 ounces cream cheese, softened
- ½ cup heavy cream
- 2 tablespoons fresh lemon juice
- 2 tablespoons honey
- Pinch of salt

Method:

1. In a bowl, add all the ingredients and mix until well combined.
2. Transfer the mixture into 2 ramekins.
3. Select "Bake" of Kalorik Digital Air Fryer Oven and then adjust the temperature to 350 degrees F.
4. Set the timer for 12 minutes and press "Start/Stop" to begin cooking.
5. When the unit beeps to show that it is preheated, place the ramekins over the air rack and insert in the Kalorik Oven.
6. When cooking time is complete, remove the ramekin from Kalorik Oven and place onto a wire rack to cool completely.
7. Refrigerate the ramekins for at least 3 hours before serving.

Nutritional Information per Serving:

- Calories 369
- Total Fat 31 g
- Saturated Fat 19.5 g
- Cholesterol 103 mg
- Sodium 261 mg
- Total Carbs 20 g
- Fiber 0.1 g
- Sugar 17.7 g
- Protein 5.1 g

Chocolate Brownies

Preparation Time: 15 minutes
Cooking Time: 15 minutes
Servings: 4

Ingredients:

- ½ cup all-purpose flour
- ¾ cup sugar
- 6 tablespoons cacao powder
- ¼ teaspoon baking powder
- ¼ teaspoon salt
- ¼ cup butter, melted
- 2 large eggs
- 1 tablespoon olive oil
- ½ teaspoon pure vanilla extract

Method:

1. Grease a 7-inch baking dish generously. Set aside.
2. In a bowl, add all the ingredients and mix until well combined.
3. Place the mixture into the prepared baking dish and with the back of a spoon, smooth the top surface.
4. Arrange the baking pan of oven in the bottom of Kalorik Digital Air Fryer Oven.
5. Select "Air Fry" of Kalorik Digital Air Fryer Oven and then adjust the temperature to 320 degrees F.
6. Set the timer for 30 minutes and press "Start/Stop" to begin cooking.
7. When the unit beeps to show that it is preheated, place the baking dish over the baking pan and insert in the Kalorik Oven.
8. When cooking time is complete, remove the pan from Kalorik Oven and place onto a wire rack to cool completely before cutting.
9. Cut the brownie into desired-sized squares and serve.

Nutritional Information per Serving:

- Calories 367
- Total Fat 19.2 g
- Saturated Fat 9.5 g
- Cholesterol 124 mg
- Sodium 265 mg
- Total Carbs 53.6 g
- Fiber 2.7 g
- Sugar 37.8 g
- Protein 6.4 g

Fruity Crumble

Preparation Time: 15 minutes
Cooking Time: 20 minutes
Servings: 4

Ingredients:

- ½ pound apple, peeled, cored and cubed
- 1 cup fresh blueberries
- 1/3 cup sugar, divided
- 1 tablespoon fresh lemon juice
- 7/8 cup all-purpose flour
- Pinch of salt
- 1 tablespoon cold water
- ¼ cup chilled butter, cubed

Method:

1. Grease a baking pan.
2. In a large bowl, add apricots, blueberries, 2 tablespoons of sugar and lemon juice and mix well.
3. Place the fruit mixture into the prepared baking pan.
4. In another bowl, add the flour, remaining sugar, salt, water, and butter and mix until a crumbly mixture form.
5. Spread the flour mixture over fruit mixture evenly.
6. Select "Air Fry" of Kalorik Digital Air Fryer Oven and then adjust the temperature to 390 degrees F.
7. Set the timer for 20 minutes and press "Start/Stop" to begin cooking.
8. When the unit beeps to show that it is preheated, place the cake pan over the air rack and insert in the Kalorik Oven.
9. When cooking time is complete, remove the pan from Kalorik Oven and place onto a wire rack to cool for about 10 minutes before serving.

Nutritional Information per Serving:

- Calories 300
- Total Fat 12 g
- Saturated 7.4 g
- Cholesterol 31 mg
- Sodium 122 mg
- Total Carbs 46.7 g
- Fiber 2.3 g
- Sugar 23.3 g
- Protein 3.3 g

Glazed Banana

Preparation Time: 10 minutes
Cooking Time: 10 minutes
Servings: 4

Ingredients:

- 2 ripe bananas, peeled and sliced lengthwise
- 1 teaspoon fresh lime juice
- 4 teaspoons maple syrup
- 1/8 teaspoon ground cinnamon

Method:

1. Coat each banana half with lime juice.
2. Arrange the banana halves onto the greased "baking pan" cut sides up.
3. Drizzle the banana halves with maple syrup and sprinkle with cinnamon.
4. Select "Air Fry" of Kalorik Digital Air Fryer Oven and then adjust the temperature to 350 degrees F.
5. Set the timer for 10 minutes and press "Start/Stop" to begin cooking.
6. When the unit beeps to show that it is preheated, insert the baking pan in the Kalorik Oven.
7. When cooking time is complete, remove the baking pan from Kalorik Oven and serve immediately.

Nutritional Information per Serving:

- Calories 70
- Total Fat 0.2 g
- Saturated Fat 0.1 g
- Cholesterol 0 mg
- Sodium 1 mg
- Total Carbs 18 g
- Fiber 1.6 g
- Sugar 11.2 g
- Protein 0.6 g

Cranberry Cupcakes

Preparation Time: 15 minutes
Cooking Time: 15 minutes
Servings: 10

Ingredients:

- 4½ ounces self-rising flour
- ½ teaspoon baking powder
- Pinch of salt
- ½ ounce cream cheese, softened
- 4¾ ounces butter, softened
- 4¼ ounces caster sugar
- 2 eggs
- 2 teaspoons fresh lemon juice
- ½ cup fresh cranberries

Method:

1. In a bowl, mix together the flour, baking powder, and salt.
2. In another bowl, mix together the cream cheese, and butter.
3. Add the sugar and beat until fluffy and light.
4. Add the eggs, one at a time and whisk until just combined.
5. Add the flour mixture and stir until well combined.
6. Stir in the lemon juice.
7. Place the mixture into silicone cups and top each with cranberries evenly, pressing slightly.
8. Select "Air Fry" of Kalorik Digital Air Fryer Oven and then adjust the temperature to 365 degrees F.
9. Set the timer for 15 minutes and press "Start/Stop" to begin cooking.
10. When the unit beeps to show that it is preheated, place the cups over the air rack and insert in the Kalorik Oven.
11. When cooking time is complete, remove the cups from Kalorik Oven and place onto a wire rack to cool for about 10 minutes.
12. Carefully, invert the cupcakes onto the wire rack to completely cool before serving.

Nutritional Information per Serving:

- Calories 209
- Total Fat 12.4 g
- Saturated Fat 7.5 g
- Cholesterol 63 mg

- Sodium 110 mg
- Total Carbs 22.6 g
- Fiber 0.6 g
- Sugar 12.4 g
- Protein 2.7 g

Apple Crisp

Preparation Time: 15 minutes
Cooking Time: 40 minutes
Servings: 2

Ingredients:

- 1½ cups apple, peeled, cored and sliced
- ¼ cup sugar, divided
- 1½ teaspoons cornstarch
- 3 tablespoons all-purpose flour
- ¼ teaspoon ground cinnamon
- Pinch of salt
- 1½ tablespoons cold butter, chopped
- 3 tablespoons rolled oats

Method:

1. In a bowl, place apple slices, 1 teaspoon of sugar and cornstarch and toss to coat well.
2. Divide the plum mixture into lightly greased 2 (8-ounce) ramekins.
3. In a bowl, mix together the flour, remaining sugar, cinnamon and salt.
4. With 2 forks, blend in the butter until a crumbly mixture forms.
5. Add the oats and gently, stir to combine.
6. Place the oat mixture over apple slices into each ramekin.
7. Select "Bake" of Kalorik Digital Air Fryer Oven and then adjust the temperature to 350 degrees F.
8. Set the timer for 40 minutes and press "Start/Stop" to begin cooking.
9. When the unit beeps to show that it is preheated, place the ramekins over the air rack and insert in the Kalorik Oven.
10. When cooking time is complete, remove the ramekins from Kalorik Oven and place onto a wire rack to cool for about 10 minutes before serving.

Nutritional Information per Serving:

- Calories 337
- Total Fat 9.6g
- Saturated Fat 5.6 g
- Cholesterol 23 mg
- Sodium 141 mg
- Total Carbs 64.3 g
- Fiber 5.3 g
- Sugar 42.5 g
- Protein 2.8 g

Zucchini Mug Cake

Preparation Time: 10 minutes
Cooking Time: 20 minutes
Serving: 1

Ingredients:

- ¼ cup whole-wheat pastry flour
- 1 tablespoon sugar
- ¼ teaspoon baking powder
- ¼ teaspoon ground cinnamon
- Pinch of salt
- 2 tablespoons plus 2 teaspoons milk
- 2 tablespoons zucchini, grated and squeezed
- 2 tablespoons almonds, chopped
- 1 tablespoon raisins
- 2 teaspoons maple syrup

Method:

1. In a bowl, mix together the flour, sugar, baking powder, cinnamon and salt.
2. Add the remaining ingredients and mix until well combined.
3. Place the mixture into a lightly greased ramekin.
4. Select "Bake" of Kalorik Digital Air Fryer Oven and then adjust the temperature to 350 degrees F.
5. Set the timer for 20 minutes and press "Start/Stop" to begin cooking.
6. When the unit beeps to show that it is preheated, place the ramekin over the air rack and insert in the Kalorik Oven.
7. When cooking time is complete, remove the ramekin from Kalorik Oven and place onto a wire rack to cool slightly before serving.

Nutritional Information per Serving:

- Calories 310
- Total Fat 7 g
- Saturated Fat 0.9 g
- Cholesterol 3 mg
- Sodium 175 mg
- Total Carbs 57.5 g
- Fiber 3.2 g
- Sugar 27.5 g
- Protein 7.2 g

Blackberry Cobbler

Preparation Time: 15 minutes
Cooking Time: 20 minutes
Servings: 6

Ingredients:

For Filling:

- 2½ cups fresh blackberries
- 1 teaspoon vanilla extract
- 1 teaspoon fresh lemon juice
- 1 cup sugar
- 1 teaspoon all-purpose flour
- 1 tablespoon butter, melted

For Topping:

- 1¾ cups all-purpose flour
- 6 tablespoons sugar
- 4 teaspoons baking powder
- 1 cup milk
- 5 tablespoons butter

For Cinnamon Sugar:

- 2 teaspoons sugar
- ¼ teaspoon ground cinnamon

Method:

1. For filling: in a bowl, add all the ingredients and mix until well combined.
2. In another large bowl, mix together the flour, baking powder, and sugar.
3. Add the milk and butter and mix until a crumbly mixture forms.
4. For cinnamon sugar: in a small bowl mix together the sugar and cinnamon.
5. In the bottom of a greased cake pan, place the blackberries mixture and top with the flour mixture evenly.
6. Sprinkle the cinnamon sugar on top evenly.
7. Arrange the baking pan of oven in the bottom of Kalorik Digital Air Fryer Oven.
8. Select "Air Fry" of Kalorik Digital Air Fryer Oven and then adjust the temperature to 320 degrees F.

9. Set the timer for 20 minutes and press "Start/Stop" to begin cooking.
10. When the unit beeps to show that it is preheated, place the cake pan over the baking pan and insert in the Kalorik Oven.
11. When cooking time is complete, remove the pan from Kalorik Oven and place onto a wire rack to cool for about 10 minutes before serving.

Nutritional Information per Serving:

- Calories 453
- Total Fat 13 g
- Saturated Fat 7.9 g
- Cholesterol 34 mg
- Sodium 106 mg
- Total Carbs 81.7 g
- Fiber 4.2 g
- Sugar 49.4 g
- Protein 6.1 g

Conclusion

The smartest Kalorik Maxx Air Fryer Oven has proven to be the most successful model of this range due to its powerful advantages: modern and multifunctional, extreme performance, large family size. The Kalorik Maxx Air Fryer Oven can do much more than you think! With this Mediterranean Kalorik Maxx Air Fryer Oven Cookbook, you can enjoy the good life of smart people.

Don't wait for another second to get this amazing cookbook now.

CPSIA information can be obtained
at www.ICGtesting.com
Printed in the USA
BVHW051000110621
609349BV00007B/2118